A GIFT FOR:

_____

FROM:

_____

DATE:

_____

# A Surrendered

## YES

## 52 DEVOTIONS TO LET GO AND LIVE FREE

## Rebekah Lyons

ZONDERVAN®

ZONDERVAN

*A Surrendered Yes*

© 2021 Rebekah Lyons

Requests for information should be addressed to:
Zondervan, *3900 Sparks Dr. SE, Grand Rapids, Michigan 49546*

ISBN 978-0-310-45757-2 (HC)
ISBN 978-0-310-45758-9 (audiobook)
ISBN 978-0-310-45755-8 (eBook)

Content excerpted from *Rhythms of Renewal*, ISBN 9780310356141, copyright © 2019 Zondervan. Used by permission. And excerpted from *You Are Free*, ISBN 9780310345527, copyright © 2017 Zondervan. Used by permission. Some content taken from *Freefall to Fly* by Rebekah Lyons. Copyright © 2013. Used by permission of Tyndale House Publishers. All rights reserved.

Unless otherwise noted, Scripture quotations are taken from The Holy Bible, New International Version®, niv®. Copyright © 1973, 1978, 1984, 2011 by Biblica, Inc.® Used by permission of Zondervan. All rights reserved worldwide. www.Zondervan.com. The "niv" and "New International Version" are trademarks registered in the United States Patent and Trademark Office by Biblica, Inc.®

Scripture quotations marked The Message are from THE MESSAGE. THE MESSAGE. Copyright © 1993, 2002, 2018 by Eugene H. Peterson. Used by permission of NavPress. All rights reserved. Represented by Tyndale House Publishers, a Division of Tyndale House Ministries.

Scripture quotations marked nkjv are from the New King James Version® © 1982 by Thomas Nelson. Used by permission. All rights reserved.

Scripture quotations marked nlt are from the Holy Bible, New Living Translation. Copyright © 1996, 2004, 2015 by Tyndale House Foundation. Used by permission of Tyndale House Ministries, Carol Stream, Illinois 60188. All rights reserved.

Any internet addresses (websites, blogs, etc.) and telephone numbers in this book are offered as a resource. They are not intended in any way to be or imply an endorsement by Zondervan, nor does Zondervan vouch for the content of these sites and numbers for the life of this book.

Author is represented by The Christopher Ferebee Agency, www.christopherferebee.com.

The Writer is represented by Cyle Young of C.Y.L.E. (Cyle Young Literary Elite, LLC), a literary agency.

Art direction: Tanamachi Studio
Interior design: Kristy Edwards

*Printed in China*

21 22 23 24 25 GRI 10 9 8 7 6 5 4 3 2 1

# Contents

*Say Yes to God*

1. God's Rescue ❧ 2
2. Healing Joy ❧ 6
3. Living Water ❧ 10
4. Declaring Truth ❧ 14
5. Who We Are ❧ 18
6. Asking the Impossible ❧ 22
7. Simply Brave ❧ 26
8. Beginning Again ❧ 30
9. God's Surprises ❧ 34
10. Letting Go ❧ 38
11. The Blessing of Friendship ❧ 42
12. Step into Adventure ❧ 46
13. New Responsibility ❧ 50
14. Restoration ❧ 55
15. Being Whole ❧ 59
16. Going Against the Grain ❧ 64
17. Mornings with God ❧ 69
18. Pulling Weeds ❧ 73

*Say Yes to Yourself*

19. Working with Your Hands ❧ 78
20. It's Okay to Say No ❧ 82
21. Expressing Your Emotions ❧ 86
22. Strength in Weakness ❧ 90
23. Rhythms of Sleep ❧ 94
24. A Little Sweat ❧ 98
25. Confession for Your Soul ❧ 102
26. The Renewal of Sabbath ❧ 106
27. Taking a Walk ❧ 110
28. Room to Breathe ❧ 114
29. Seasons of Rest ❧ 119
30. Something New ❧ 123
31. Dreaming Dreams ❧ 127
32. Healthy Play ❧ 131
33. Taking a Risk ❧ 135
34. Creating Beauty ❧ 139
35. New Learning ❧ 143
36. Holy Inventory ❧ 147
37. Turn Off the Tech ❧ 151
38. Your Calling ❧ 155

*Say Yes to Others*

39.  Set Free ≈ 160

40.  The Way of Forgiveness ≈ 164

41.  The Gift of Hugs ≈ 168

42.  I'm Sorry ≈ 172

43.  Open Porches and Open Doors ≈ 176

44.  Welcoming Vulnerability ≈ 180

45.  Extravagant Love ≈ 184

46.  True Connection ≈ 189

47.  A Quiet Stillness ≈ 194

48.  Heart Work ≈ 198

49.  Bearing Another's Burdens ≈ 202

50.  Surrendering Power ≈ 206

51.  Making Memories ≈ 211

52.  Celebrate Freedom ≈ 215

*Notes* ≈ 219

*About the Author* ≈ 227

# Say

# to God

# God's Rescue

He rescued me because he delighted in me.

PSALM 18:19

Gabe was first to catch the itch to move to New York City. He reasoned that it was the perfect home for Q, the organization we had started to equip Christians to engage in our culture. I resisted for three years; how could a Southern girl leave Atlanta for New York City? Finally I relented. We loaded three kids and two toy poodles into our minivan (a vehicle that is not hip anywhere but is especially uncool when pulling into midtown Manhattan).

I thought New York would bring new adventure. Instead, I found myself melting down. I was on an airplane over New York during my first panic attack; fear closed in, threatened to capsize everything. This first bout of anxiety set in motion a cycle that could not be reversed.

*Anxiety became my fancy word for fear.*

The panic took over in trains, subways, elevators, and crowds. If you've visited Manhattan (or any large metropolis, for that matter), you know it's impossible to avoid these things. One day, panic set in as the subway doors closed. I tried to pry them apart, clawing at them with my hands. But the train took off anyway with me trapped inside it, engulfed in hot tears and desperate prayers.

> Anxiety became my fancy word for fear.

My anxiety attacks continued for almost a year. One Tuesday morning, friends gathered to pray that I would be delivered from fear and panic. Late that night, I woke as I'd done so many times before, unable to breathe, unable to speak. I could only grip my husband's arms while he interceded for me. Finally I found my voice and confessed my desperate need:

"God, rescue me; deliver me; I cannot do this without you."

In an instant my panic evaporated. My once shaking body grew calm. My breathing became normal, and my heart stopped racing. In more charismatic circles, people would say God healed me instantly, but this Baptist girl had no language for it.

Up until the moment God set me free from panic attacks,

I did not believe I could be healed of depression and panic. I remembered how I tiptoed out of my apartment later that day, cautious and unsure. Did the healing really take?

The city burst into living color as October trees lined the mall of Central Park with oranges, golds, and reds. And my soul came alive again. I stayed in the present, absorbed each sunrise and sunset. *Is this what rebirth feels like?* I pondered.

With a bit of trepidation, I began to share my story with close friends. As I shared my story, women responded, seeming to feel permission to be honest about their struggles. I caught a glimpse of God waking others to his desire and ability to meet them in their places of need. And I realized, *this wasn't my story of struggle; it was his story of rescue.*

I wondered, *could God use this to bring freedom to others?* This was uncharted territory, but I was ready to follow the path he'd chosen. I trusted God would take my hand. He would lead and guide me.

# ❧ Reflect ❧

WE ALL HAVE THINGS IN OUR LIVES FROM WHICH WE NEED
RESCUE, WHETHER IT'S FEAR, HEALTH ISSUES, GRIEF, OR SOME-
THING ELSE ALTOGETHER. SPEND SOME TIME JOURNALING
ABOUT THIS NEED IN YOUR LIFE. CONFESS TO GOD YOUR NEED
FOR HIS RESCUE AND HEALING.

# Healing Joy

"These things I have spoken to
you, that my joy may be in you,
and that your joy may be full."

JOHN 15:11 ESV

I 'll never forget the day I realized I'd lost my joy.

Somewhere in the clouds over Colorado, my son Pierce and I huddled watching a slideshow on my laptop. Hundreds of images depicting our family's history rolled across the screen:

Gabe and I as newlyweds.

The wonder in our eyes as new parents.

Pierce giggling and tugging on Cade as the two waddled around the room.

The arrival of our third blessing, Kennedy.

Images of pumpkin patches, Easter egg hunts, and pool parties.

Laughter and light had been captured by the camera lens through the years. Suddenly, I saw a single tear stream down Pierce's cheek.

"What is it, son?"

"You seem to have lost your joy since we were little," he said. "You don't smile like that anymore."

I wanted to weep. I'd had no idea my internal struggle was so noticeable. No joy for my children to see? This was too much.

*Lord, you could not have staged a more powerful intervention.*

I pondered the words our children heard from me on a daily basis.

"Hurry up!"

"Stop fighting!"

"Clean your room!"

> No joy for my children to see? This was too much.

The negativity of my own words turned into a pounding gavel in my head. When had I stopped nurturing my children?

When I had a chance, I stole away to a private place. I paused. Sat still. Listened. As I prayed, God revealed that my lack of joy sprang from feelings of insecurity—feelings I'd denied out of a desire to appear confident and together. I confessed, *Why do I run so hard when I have already earned your unconditional love? Oh, the joy-robbing sadness of striving. Please restore to me the joy of my salvation.*

I knew the truth—God loved me as I was. He paid the price to set me free, and he wanted me to take joy in my freedom. He wanted me to feel free to celebrate.

A few weeks later, I walked through the park on an early spring day with crystal-clear skies and tulips practically bursting into bloom. In prayer, I listened and heard God whispering that he'd come "to seek and to save the lost."[1] Something was happening. Joy was growing in me.

Eugene Peterson said, "*Salvation* means the healing and rescue of a body that is brought back to the way it was intended."[2] Salvation is not just for our souls; it's for every part of our lives.

My attitude began to shift. I started speaking new life into my kids, birthed from a place of joy:

"You are my beloved."

"We will face your fears together."

"You were meant for amazing things."

"I will nurture the talents God has planted in you."

It took walking through my own wilderness to learn the true source of joy. *The joy of Christ becomes our joy.* I cannot fathom the kindness of Jesus—how he turns all our mourning into dancing. I was free to celebrate because even on the toughest days, I could claim the promise of the cross and resurrection.

# ✺ Reflect ✺

JOY IS NOT THE ABSENCE OF DARKNESS. JOY IS CONFIDENCE
THAT THE DARKNESS WILL LIFT. ARE YOU LIVING IN THE JOY
AND CELEBRATION GOD HAS FREED YOU TO LIVE IN? READ THE
WORDS OF PSALM 139, AND ASK GOD TO REVEAL THE PLACES
IN YOUR LIFE THAT ARE IN NEED OF HEALING. ASK HIM TO LEAD
YOU TO JOY, AND THEN WATCH FOR THE WAYS HE ANSWERS YOU.

# 3

# Living Water

"If you only knew the gift God has for you
and who you are speaking to, you would
ask me, and I would give you living water."

JOHN 4:10 NLT

We are hardwired to thirst. In fact, thirst is said to be the strongest of all human urges. When we are thirsty, we will do anything to be filled.

How much do I thirst for God?

Do I ache for him?

Long for his presence?

Desire his peace?

Burn for his compassion?

Like the children of Israel, I'd spent years in the wilderness—

spiritually dry and thirsty, looking to the wrong things to satisfy my longings, to be considered worthy. Growing up in church, I did my best to obey all the right rules. When I failed, God seemed far off, and I felt undeserving of his love. The God I imagined shook his head in disappointment when in reality his arms were spread wide, longing to satisfy the spiritual thirst of his daughter.

I confessed to Jesus,

> *I'm one of the broken ones, you know.*
> *For years I've loved seas and rivers, always drawn to the water.*
> *But you are the living water, poured out readily as a healing balm whenever I come.*
> *You are the bread of life that hung on a cross.*
> *You uttered, "I am thirsty," even then, for my freedom.*
> *Help me thirst for you in return.*
> *Heal me in places I don't even know I need healing.*
> *Show me what you see.*
> *Show me what you want to set free.*

I couldn't help but remember the woman at the well in John 4. Like me, she didn't know *how* to thirst for living water. She didn't even know she wanted it until Jesus pointed it out to her. He said,

"When you drink the water I give you, you'll never be thirsty again." She immediately replied, "How do I get this water?"[1]

Jesus prompted her thirst then. He prompts our thirst now.

Growing up, I never understood my longing for approval was really an unquenched thirst for Jesus and his unconditional love for me. But he came to me just as he came to the woman at the well and offered me the waters of life. Those waters, I discovered, were a bubbling spring from *within me*. This spring of life quenched my thirst for love and acceptance.

> **My longing for approval was really an unquenched thirst for Jesus and his unconditional love for me.**

I'd tried to quench my thirst for the goodness of God by drinking the world's water, but I could never get enough. The world's water only created more drought and famine.

Instead, I needed to learn a holier thirst, the thirst for the presence of God, for revival, for small ministry in the church. I needed more of his goodness, not more of the world's acclaim, and I hoped to carry this goodness to a world thirsting for the same thing. I'd known I wanted Jesus to revive his church, but I now realized revival began in individual hearts. I asked him to revive *me*. Will you join me in asking Jesus to revive you, to quench your thirst with his living water?

# Reflect

ARE YOU THIRSTY? ARE YOU TRYING TO QUENCH THAT THIRST WITH THE THINGS OF THIS WORLD, THE APPROVAL OF OTHERS, OR WITH THE LIVING WATER OF CHRIST? JOURNAL YOUR THOUGHTS, CONFESSING FREELY THE THINGS YOU NEED TO CHANGE. THEN ASK JESUS TO QUENCH YOUR THIRST WITH HIS LIVING WATER.

# 4

# Declaring Truth

"But what about you?" [Jesus]
asked. "Who do you say I am?"

MATTHEW 16:15

I f we want to be free, we have to move beyond confessing our need for forgiveness and healing. We also have to believe and confess this truth: Christ came, walked this earth, paid the price, bought us, and set us free. He declares, "You are free; be who you already are."

Most of us understand confession as a form of repentance, an admission of guilt and a request for forgiveness and healing. But confession has another meaning as well, one just as essential on our journey to freedom. Confession can also mean *declaring something emphatically*, such as our faith. Romans 10:9 says, "If you confess with your mouth the Lord Jesus . . . that God has raised Him from the dead, you will be saved."[1]

When we confess something with our mouths, we plant truth deep in our hearts. It becomes a seed, eventually yielding a harvest. Faith is always the evidence of what we can't yet see; faith trusts what Jesus declares is true. Confession, then, is a specific form of faith.

*Confession begins with repentance and ends with declaration.*

We trust that even in the darkness of our own unbelief and sin, we'll look back years later and see how faith exploded from a mustard seed into a freedom song, a healing song.

Jesus doesn't say you *can* be or *may* be or *will* be free. He says you *are* free.[2] Therefore, we must declare—we must confess—truths like the following:

> Jesus doesn't say you *can* be or *may* be or *will* be free. He says you *are* free.

- We are adopted heirs of the throne, sons and daughters of a King.[3]
- His love knows no bounds.[4] It is an everlasting, all-consuming fire invading our hearts and minds when we allow it, and it turns our worlds upside down.[5]
- No amount of loss or sadness or rejection separates us from his great and marvelous love.[6]

- No amount of manipulating and toiling, of approval seeking, will ever increase his love for us or bring us into right relationship with Jesus.
- *Freedom has already come.*[7] It is found at the foot of the cross, where Christ took our lack on himself and declared, "I am enough. I have bought you with a price and set you free."[8]

My family will attest that I fall short of God's glory every single day, but my understanding of my freedom has completely changed:

*The fall may be everywhere around us, but it is not in us.*

*Instead, it is Christ in us, the hope of glory.*

Isn't this the point of the good news? When we confess our brokenness and receive the full pardon of Jesus, we are free.

Many in the church cannot fathom the kind of freedom Christ's pardon brings. We are so used to our prison cells, we don't even know we are still in them! The doors are wide open—Christ tore them off the hinges two thousand years ago. Many of us, though, still stand inside. Are you ready to step outside?

# ❧ Reflect ❧

ARE YOU STILL STUCK IN AN OPEN PRISON CELL? ARE YOU
READY TO STEP THROUGH THE DOOR? TO HELP YOU ON YOUR
JOURNEY, BEGIN A LIST OF THE VERSES THAT DECLARE WHO YOU
ARE IN CHRIST. WRITE OUT THE TRUTHS YOU NEED TO HEAR AND
REMEMBER, AND REFER TO THEM OFTEN.

# 5

# Who We Are

You created my inmost being; you knit me
together in my mother's womb. I praise you
because I am fearfully and wonderfully made;
your works are wonderful, I know that full well.

PSALM 139:13–14

Mom, what is Down syndrome?" Pierce asked with tear-stained, chubby cheeks after exiting the bus one autumn day in second grade. The term for his brother's medical diagnosis had yet to surface in our home. We weren't in denial as parents; we simply wanted our younger two to know their brother for all he is, as Cade.

When Pierce and Kennedy were in first grade and pre-K, friends sometimes noticed something different about Cade and asked them about it. In "big" brother fashion, Pierce would respond, "That's Cade. He learns differently than some kids. Sometimes he just needs extra time." This seemed to satisfy the curious observers. After all, those inquiring were often children of our family friends, and they'd always known Cade as happy, great at dancing and hugs, all of which earned high praise in toddlerland.

Things took a turn when we moved to New York City.

That autumn day, as I explained that Cade had Down syndrome, I realized that information wasn't what our kids were after. They had a bigger question on their minds: Was something *wrong* with Cade?

Wanting to give these brave hearts the answers they needed, I paused for a silent prayer. I told them the label "Down syndrome" was a way of explaining to the world how Cade's body works, but it doesn't define Cade. Cade is Cade. To capstone the moment, I asked, "Aren't we glad God saw fit to let us be his family?" Without hesitation, both kids nodded in vigorous support.

Once you know someone, you no longer label them.

I've been struck by how many conversations revolve around our labels. "I'm ADD, OCD, manic, depressed, disabled, handicapped, diabetic . . ." The list goes on and on. The problem is, these labels often give us our deepest sense of identity.

> Once you know someone, you no longer label them.

But what if we came to understand that labels don't define us? That, instead, they are an explanation to help the world understand things we've dealt with or come up against? When we don't view our identity through a label, we're able to find ways to thrive in spite of whatever label we are living under.

The Christian faith leads us to an identity rooted in something more solid, more trustworthy, more immovable than the world's labels—God himself. When I need to be reminded of who I really am, I read this list of phrases from God's truth, and it always helps:

I am a child of God. (John 1:12)
I am a friend of Jesus. (John 15:15)
I am created by God to do good. (Ephesians 2:10)
I am free in Christ. (Galatians 5:1)
I am chosen and loved. (1 Thessalonians 1:4)
I am the light of the world. (Matthew 5:14)
I am not ruled by fear. (2 Timothy 1:7)
I am forgiven. (Colossians 2:13)
I am secure in him. (1 Peter 1:3–5)

Take a moment to ask God who you are in him, and root yourself deep in that identity. Then, go out into the world, secure and confident in who you really are.

## Reflect

LIST THE LABELS YOU ARE LIVING UNDER—BOTH THE LABELS
GIVEN TO YOU BY YOURSELF AND BY OTHERS. STUDY THE LIST OF
SCRIPTURES ON THE PREVIOUS PAGE. WHICH OF THOSE LABELS
MOST RESONATES WITH YOU? HOW WOULD APPLYING THAT
GOD-GIVEN LABEL TO YOUR LIFE CHANGE THE WAY YOU SEE
YOURSELF AND OTHERS?

# 6

# Asking the Impossible

Jesus looked at them and said, "With
man this is impossible, but with
God all things are possible."

MATTHEW 19:26

Sometime after God healed me from the panic attacks and
anxiety that had plagued my early days in New York, I was
answering questions publicly during an evening service. The
moderator's penetrating questions made me feel uneasy. She
wanted to talk more, and she pressed in.

Was I really healed?

What did I think about healing?

Did I have a theological framework for it?

The Baptist girl in me squirmed. Finally, I told the audience,

"I've never publicly talked about this because I know the discussion of healing is fraught with baggage. But if anyone here would like prayer for healing—spiritual, physical, mental, emotional—just ask. I'd be honored to pray with you."

I followed this with a shrug of my shoulders, a half smile, and this disclaimer: "I'm not promising anything, but it never hurts to ask."

Sheepish grins and muffled laughter filled the room. The session ended, and I was sure everyone would exit as quickly as possible. Instead, women began to line up along the aisles and the back of the room. Looking back, I see how that night marked a change in the way God had called me to minister.

What if disciple-making is not just talking *about God* but inviting others to talk *to God*? What if disciple-making is about giving people the freedom to ask, no matter how big or impossible the request? Because here's the key:

*We aren't responsible for the healing (or whatever seemingly impossible thing we are asking for); we're only responsible for the asking.*

Then comes the tricky part. After we ask comes the silence, the waiting, and the questions: Will we wait for God? Will we trust him?

Maybe you've asked God for

> **What if disciple-making is not just talking *about God* but inviting others to talk *to God*?**

something but heard only silence for many years, and it feels like your mustard seed of faith isn't growing.[1] Maybe you've felt faithless and condemned, abandoned and rejected.

I don't know why God answers some prayers immediately and not others. It's a mystery. What I do know with full assurance is this: God has given us the freedom to ask him for anything— *anything*. Perhaps in God's economy what's most important is that we have the freedom and faith to ask.

Asking says, "I cannot fathom how you would do this, but I trust you are able. So I lay aside what I can understand, and I embrace your promise and mystery of healing."

Being free to ask God for anything means trusting him the way a child trusts—openly and unreservedly and expectantly. It means not holding back. And isn't that the crux of our faith?

The asking—sometimes it's the hardest part. Do you feel this? We second-guess God's love, his faithfulness, his power to heal, restore, and provide. But Scripture teaches us to ask. In Luke we're taught, "For everyone who asks receives; the one who seeks finds; and to the one who knocks, the door will be opened."[2]

Maybe you've never experienced the freedom to ask for healing and wholeness. Maybe you've second-guessed the power of God. But God our Father responds with love, power, and healing. Invite God to visit you in your need. Just ask.

# ∞ Reflect ∞

WHAT DO YOU MOST NEED IN YOUR LIFE RIGHT NOW? WRITE OUT A PRAYER ASKING GOD TO BLESS YOUR LIFE WITH WHATEVER IT IS YOU ARE NEEDING, NO MATTER HOW IMPOSSIBLE IT MAY SEEM. FINISH YOUR PRAYER WITH A DECLARATION OF YOUR FAITH AND TRUST IN HIM. WHAT'S ONE REQUEST THAT SEEMS TOO FOOLISH TO ASK? IS THERE AN AREA OF LIFE WHERE YOU'VE LOST HOPE THAT GOD REALLY CARES?

# 7

# Simply Brave

*He who began a good work in you will carry it*
*on to completion until the day of Christ Jesus.*

PHILIPPIANS 1:6

T he first time I ever spoke in public was at a writing workshop, six months before my first book was released. When I stepped up to the microphone, I said, verbatim, "This is the first and last time I'll be speaking in public, so here goes." (In hindsight, I don't recommend this.)

I proceeded to cry through my story, sniffling into tissues, ending my time with a rousing offer to pray. To my surprise, at the end of my session, about fifteen women formed a line to talk. My story had touched them, had offered them something they needed. I'd given language to anxiety and depression, something not often talked about in church. I left hoping to get the chance to speak again.

The speaking invitations crept in. But speaking brought fear, so I'd write out my talks word for word, only to find myself speaking with my head down, following the script too closely. If I looked up to reference a slide, I'd lose my place in my notes.

A few months into this new vocation, I found myself on an airplane headed to give three forty-five-minute talks at a conference. This time, due to weather, my flight was running behind. I had only thirty minutes to make my connection in Atlanta's Hartsfield-Jackson Airport—one of the busiest in the world. I ran from concourse to train to concourse and was the last to board for the final leg of the trip. As we reached ten thousand feet, I leaned down to get my laptop and put a few finishing touches on my upcoming talks.

*My laptop was still in the seat pocket of my last flight.*

I arrived at my hotel in a puddle of exhaustion, fear, and frustration. Now what? No notes, no computer. Falling to my knees, I confessed right then:

*Never have I wanted my teaching to be about what I bring. I don't want my words to be my own, my talks to be controlled or predictable. But I'm afraid not to plan every word.*

*Will you please help me? Speak through me? Surprise us all with what you have?*

God gently responded: "Do you trust me? Do you trust I will give you my words?"

God was looking for this little girl to simply be brave. I taught three sessions without notes that weekend. It was the most free I'd ever felt standing in front of a group of women. As it turns out, I love telling stories on the fly.

> God was looking for this little girl to simply be brave.

It's difficult to muster bravery in our everyday lives, isn't it? So often, fear creeps in. *What if I fail? What if others ridicule me?* Our emotions are very real, and I do not wish to minimize them. But our bravest moments come from trusting, from falling into the plan of God. When we do, bravery becomes less about courage and more about faith. We trust God will never leave us or forsake us.[1] We trust everything is possible for those who believe.[2] We trust we can do all things through Christ, who gives us strength.[3] He is faithful to accomplish whatever he begins and will carry it to completion.[4]

# ✺ Reflect ✺

REFLECT ON THE PAST MONTH AND IDENTIFY A MOMENT WHEN YOU SHRANK BACK FROM WHAT YOU WANTED TO DO, EITHER AT HOME OR IN THE WORKPLACE OR IN YOUR COMMUNITY. SPEND SOME TIME REFLECTING ON WHAT UNDERLYING FEARS CAUSED YOU TO WITHHOLD YOURSELF. IDENTIFY OPPORTUNITIES TO TRY AGAIN WITHIN THE COMING MONTH. ENGAGE YOUR BRAVEST SELF, KNOWING THAT GOD SUSTAINS AND UPHOLDS YOU.

# 8

# Beginning Again

"Anyone who loves me will obey my teaching.
My Father will love them, and we will come
to them and make our home with them."

JOHN 14:23

Gabe and I were ready for radical change, so we sold the majority of our possessions and moved from Atlanta to Manhattan. In the beginning it felt freeing—the maintenance of our things felt suffocating—but ridding myself of the comfort of the familiar also left me without a safety net, forcing me to see the truth: my soul was bankrupt. In the South, I'd leaned so heavily on stable friendships and an established home that when they were yanked away, I was lost. Overwhelmed by this reality, I begged God to return things to the way they'd been. Seller's remorse.

Sometimes it takes being stripped of what is familiar to be reminded of who we truly are. Under his watchful keeping, God used New York City to show me I'm brave and independent. Falling isn't so scary once you lean into the wind. After all, that's how baby birds learn to fly; they free fall to fly.

Over time, Gabe and I learned to thrive in New York, but the same could not be said of our three kids. We'd been in New York for four years when Cade suddenly wouldn't get out of bed in the mornings. A social bug, he'd always leapt out of bed, excited for the school day. I grew concerned when his reluctance to go to school continued day after day

> **Falling isn't so scary once you lean into the wind.**

after day. And Kennedy and Pierce were facing their own challenges. Kids teased Pierce if he mentioned God. When Kennedy was called "sexy" on her first day of second grade, I had to ponder whether the New York life was sustainable for all five of us.

As we considered where we might plant our family for the years to come, Nashville, Tennessee, kept moving to the top of the list. But my first reaction was *no*. Don't get me wrong. The horse farms outside of Nashville are dreamy, and the rolling hills are picturesque, but I couldn't accept the thought of starting over again. I was afraid the comfort of the South would cause me to feel complacent. The truth is, I had yet to experience a vibrant daily relationship with God that wasn't tethered to struggle, and the struggle of New York City was palpable. What would happen to my faith in the comfort of Christianville?

I committed the matter to prayer and confessed, *I'm afraid to begin again, to risk again in a new city. Is this the right decision? Help me see what you see.*

I listened for God's whispers. He gently reminded me that my free fall into his grace was not because of New York but because of *him*. Manhattan was only the setting. God assured me that what he began there—my confession, his bending low—was a union, and he could continue it anywhere.

I could run from city to city, apartment to apartment, opportunity to opportunity looking for *home*. But the only home that will *keep* me is Jesus, safe in his arms. He'll make home with me, whether I am in Nashville, Manhattan, or Timbuktu. Wherever I make my bed, he'll be there.

This is the beauty of our God. *He is our home.*

# Reflect

THINK ABOUT THE WORD *HOME*. WHAT IMAGES AND EMOTIONS, WHAT MEMORIES AND LONGINGS DOES THAT WORD EVOKE? HAVE YOU FOUND YOUR TRUE HOME? AND IF NOT, WHAT STEP CAN YOU TAKE TODAY TO REORIENT YOURSELF TO HIM?

# 9

# God's Surprises

May the God of peace . . . equip you with
everything good for doing his will.

HEBREWS 13:20–21

I love reading about Moses' first encounter with the God of the universe in a burning bush. The dialogue between them makes me laugh because Moses' objections remind me of my own.

> GOD: Go to Pharaoh so you can bring my people out of Egypt.
>
> MOSES: What? Who, me?
>
> GOD: I will be with you.
>
> MOSES: What if they ask who sent me?
>
> GOD: I Am has sent you.

MOSES: What if they don't believe me?

GOD: I'll give you the power to perform signs and wonders in my name.

MOSES: But I'm not good with words.

This is where I can imagine God saying slowly and firmly, "Moses, who made your mouth? Go! I'll help you speak, and I'll tell you what to say."[1]

It's easy to read about Moses' doubt and think, *This is God speaking to you! Don't you trust him?* Then I think of all the times I've determined God must have confused his plans for me with his plans for someone else. I've offered up plenty of *I can't do this! Just look at my mess!* I wonder what God thinks as he listens to my fears of never-enough-ness.

God does the choosing and assigning, not us. Whew! He calls us, and he equips us. There's no need to run from his calling, to deny it, or to wish it away because "the God of peace, who through the blood of the eternal covenant brought back from the dead our Lord Jesus, that great Shepherd of the sheep," will also "equip [us] with everything good for doing his will."[2]

God demonstrates his power through our frailty. In fact, this is the only thing we can boast in: *His power is made perfect and on full display in our never-enough-ness.* When we are weak, we are actually made strong in Christ Jesus.[3]

Whoa. *The secret to strength is weakness.*

Grasping this has been a game changer for me. I used to think being ill-equipped disqualified me from serving God, but I've learned that when I admit my inadequacy, I invite his power in to strengthen me. This is fertile soil for surrender. Surrender says, *The calling you've laid before me is too great. I cannot fathom it. Still, I will obey. I will trust that you go before me.*

> God demonstrates his power through our frailty.

I believe God chose Moses *because* he was weak. God wanted Moses to know he was able to lead the people only because God was with him, giving him everything he needed to do the job.

When you feel weak—or anxious or fearful—the very admission of your weakness could be the moment you realize true strength. And in that moment, you'll see that you are the one God wants to use. You're it. God's glory rests in *you.*

What joy to come before the throne, humbled and low. What freedom to be used, shortcomings and all. This is when we realize that we, *the weak ones*, have been a part of God's plan all along.

## ✥ Reflect ✥

HAVE YOU FOUND YOURSELF BELIEVING THAT PAST MISTAKES OR EVEN CURRENT SITUATIONS DISQUALIFY YOU FROM BEING USED BY GOD? HOW MIGHT THOSE SAME THINGS BE PART OF THE VERY REASON GOD CHOOSES TO USE YOU IN HIS KINGDOM?

# 10

# Letting Go

"But seek first his kingdom and his
righteousness, and all these things
will be given to you as well."

MATTHEW 6:33

Moving day was just two weeks away, and we still didn't have a place to live in Nashville. For the past three months, we'd exhausted ourselves searching for an apartment. When bedtime came one night, I considered staying up late to journal my troubles. (Writing usually grants me insight I don't find any other way.) However, fatigue won. I couldn't move another muscle and offered a request to the heavens. *God, please show up in my sleep.* I closed my eyes and immediately heard, "The LORD is my shepherd; I shall not want."[1]

*I shall not want.* For anything? What about a place to rent?

The truth is, I wasn't merely waiting for the ideal housing situation. I was waiting for an answer to a larger question: What was the point of all the moving? Leaving Atlanta for New York City, then leaving New York City for Nashville, I felt caught in a loop. I wouldn't understand for a good long while, but in waiting on God for a simple apartment, he was showing me I had to wait on his timing for *everything*.

We arrived in Nashville on a sweltering Monday in August. And over the course of a morning, I received multiple texts from local friends offering to help. We were in the South again, and I felt it. Our friends worked quickly, and by dinner our closets were filled and our cabinets were organized. Yet I mentally compared this moving day with the day we unloaded our truck onto the Upper East Side. Moving felt like a beginning on that day, but today it felt like an ending.

During the weeks that followed, I watched as Gabe and the children flourished. But me, I drove my minivan like a martyr. To the grocery store, to carpool, to the gym, declaring under my breath that this move would be great for everyone but me. Then one Tuesday morning, as I was having breakfast with a new friend, she said, "Perhaps God has called you to something, and he's holding it off for a reason?" Tears began streaming from my eyes as I pondered her question. Then the answer came:

> I watched as Gabe and the children flourished. But me, I drove my minivan like a martyr.

*You cannot see the unknown until you release the known.*

It hit me; I needed to *let go* of New York. All I saw was scarcity because I was not seeing the transition, the waiting, as gifts from God.

The life of the believer hangs in the balance between the now and the not yet. We can know the call of God on our lives and feel anxious to get to it, but God sometimes calls us to wait as he refines us, as he shows himself to be our redeemer, rescuer, and healer. We must confess that his timing is best, and trust and declare that the waiting will bring us into a place of readiness.

Perhaps you are in a time of waiting. You straddle promise and doubt, feebly holding on to the hope of promise. Keep holding on. You may not know the outcome, but you can rest in the tension of the waiting. It's in the tension that the music is made.

There will come a moment when God says, "It's time." Just wait and see.

# Reflect

ARE YOU IN A TIME OF WAITING, A TIME OF "NOT YET"? MIGHT IT BE BECAUSE GOD IS WAITING FOR YOU TO LET GO OF SOMETHING ELSE FIRST? LOOK FOR WAYS HE IS EQUIPPING, TRAINING, AND PREPARING YOU DURING THIS TIME—WHAT DO YOU SEE?

# 11

# The Blessing of Friendship

"And as you wish that others would
do to you, do so to them."

LUKE 6:31 ESV

As we arrived at our new home in Nashville, shiny keys in hand, I noticed a large bag hanging from the front door. Was this our first housewarming gift? I jogged to the door to peek inside the bag. Inside were hundreds of colorful bows of all shapes and sizes—nothing but bows. I opened the attached note and read: "Put these bows on all of your moving boxes and tell your kids it's Christmas. It makes unpacking way more fun! Love you, Elisabeth." It was just a little note, but a warm reminder that three years in, Nashville had become home. Forging friendships in a new community takes time, and it isn't always easy.

Just a couple of years prior, I had awakened to the realization that I was lonely and disconnected. At the age of forty, rebuilding community and deep friendships was a different ball game than it had been in my twenties. Everyone was busy and saddled with the responsibilities that come with careers and kids. What's more, they had plenty of time-honored friendships and weren't looking to add more cookouts, birthday parties, or dinner dates to the calendar. It wasn't just them, though. On many weekends my work took me out of town, so I missed out on supper clubs and church events, all the places where new friendship could be forged.

And though God had blessed me with beautiful, open, and honest friendships over the years, there was another side to friendship too. I had two friends who bailed in hard seasons: one in my twenties, one in my thirties. Both times I was left wondering, *What is wrong with me?*

This anxiety bled into my other relationships. If a friend commented that I was too vulnerable, I would rein it in. Too serious, I'd lighten up. Too passionate, I'd get silly. I'd change anything so as not to lose another friend. Dancing on eggshells, I was afraid to be myself. I started questioning, *Am I too much or not enough?*

One day I called a long-distance friend of twenty years, Trina, and after I spilled my guts, she reminded me of an axiom she lives by: Be the friend you wish to have.

It really is that simple.

So I decided to make some changes. I'd let down the walls and be open to whomever God brought my way. I began taking fewer engagements and created more margin in my calendar. I stopped adjusting who I am in order to satisfy others.

**Be the friend you wish to have.**

As I set out to *be the friend I wanted to have*, I found I was cultivating deep friendships, friendships that were easy and covered with grace. When I stopped focusing on myself, when I focused on how I could love friends well, encourage them, and show up for their most important moments and needs, everything changed.

What if we let God be in charge of our friendships? What if we trusted that he places the right people in our lives at the right times? When we're authentic, when we bless and love, we find a community of love. It's this community that gives us the courage to go out into the world as the blessing we were made to be. Reach out. Be intentional. Be the friend you wish to have.

# Reflect

HOW ARE THE FRIENDSHIPS IN YOUR LIFE? WHICH FRIENDSHIPS ARE CAUSING YOU STRESS, ANXIETY? WHICH OFFER ENCOURAGEMENT AND PEACE? WHAT CAN YOU DO THIS WEEK TO BE THE FRIEND YOU WANT TO HAVE IN YOUR LIFE? PERHAPS WRITE YOUR FRIEND A HANDWRITTEN LETTER OR PROVIDE HER DINNER THROUGH AN APP.

# 12

## Step into Adventure

"Call to me and I will answer you
and tell you great and unsearchable
things you do not know."

JEREMIAH 33:3

A year ago, Gabe and I marked our twentieth year of marriage with a celebratory trip to Europe. The time away from kids and responsibilities felt like a honeymoon.

We woke in Lauterbrunnen, Switzerland, and had planned a rigorous hike in the Alps for our first day to get the blood flowing. But of course I didn't quite think through the requirements. To get to the trailhead, halfway up the mountain, we'd need a different form of transportation. After we scooped up our tickets at the counter and headed up an escalator, we came upon a platform with a glass box—a green gondola—ready to soar high in the sky.

At least fifty people were already jammed inside, and it was suspended in the air by a mere cable. Gabe, knowing my struggles with heights and tight spaces, asked, "You want to wait thirty minutes for the next shuttle? I'm happy to wait. But there's no guarantee there will be less people on the next round." My mind raced, recalling countless other times I'd jumped off overcrowded elevators and subways before the doors closed, my confidence evaporating. Tears began to well in the corners of my eyes.

I took a deep breath and responded, "I need this to be a week wherein I am brave. I cannot miss these moments because I'm gripped with fear. Let's do this."

I held my breath as the doors slammed shut. As the tram made its trip, I whispered Jesus' name over and over. If bravery is moving scared, this was the only way I knew to keep going.

> "I need this to be a week wherein I am brave."

As we approached the mountain ridge platform, I felt the exhilaration of relief. We shot from that glass box like a cannon, courageous and free! The ensuing hike was glorious. Taking in these majestic mountain moments felt extra special due to my bravery. Little steps of courage gave way to a week of adventure.

Following our stay in Switzerland, we rented a car and ventured onto the road. We drove through Geneva. We explored waterfront cities and marinas in Italy. We climbed rocks and jumped off cliffs and swam in the Mediterranean. We even rented a speedboat at Lake Como for some fun in the sun. It was a very active, thrilling, magical week.

Determined not to be overcome by fear, I'd stepped into adventure and loved it!

Fear holds us back and keeps us believing the lie that we aren't strong enough, brave enough, or mentally tough enough to break out of our ruts, even when we know better. But by reminding ourselves of the truth (this elevator won't fall to the ground; there's nothing to worry about in this small space) and pushing into adventure, we can regain control over fear.

If we are creative beings, dependent on imagination, doesn't it ring true that when we foster new experiences, we'll feel alive? Anything can be made into an adventure. Take your family or a few friends for a weekend camping expedition. Visit a local art gallery or go on an architecture tour of your city. Set out to expose yourself to new things, especially if the adventure requires you to overcome a fear or two.

# ⇘ Reflect ⇙

ARE FEARS KEEPING YOU FROM EXPERIENCING THE JOYS OF ADVENTURE IN YOUR LIFE? HOW MIGHT PUSHING YOURSELF TO TAKE AN ADVENTURE ACTUALLY HELP YOU OVERCOME FEAR? PLAN AN ADVENTURE THIS WEEK—NO MATTER HOW BIG OR SMALL—PREFERABLY ONE THAT ENCOURAGES YOU TO FACE ONE OF YOUR FEARS.

# 13

# New Responsibility

Whatever you do, work at it with all
your heart, as working for the Lord.

COLOSSIANS 3:23

We were returning from our annual retreat—the one where Gabe and I spend a few days alone, *sans* children, forgetting anything that reminds us of our frenetic lives. As we walked up to the door to greet our children, I looked down and saw white feathers strewn everywhere. Clearly, we'd just stepped into a fresh and savage crime scene. The victim: one of our five-month-old chickens. As I followed the feather trail into the woods, I knew we were lucky that only one of our dozen had become a feast for the raccoon family camping in our woods.

As I glanced over to the coop, the door appeared to be unlatched and hanging open.

Now, there aren't many animals cuter than yellow, fluffy baby chickens. Until this year, I'd only observed these cuties on the web or in a children's petting zoo. But that all changed when Kennedy decided she wanted to participate in our county's 4-H project. The project? Raise a dozen hens from birth to six months old, then auction off five at the county fair. The payoff? We keep a few hens and eat lots of omelets, scrambled eggs, and breakfasts for dinner!

There was a bigger reason we said yes to chickens, though, and it had to do with anxiety. Not mine, but Kennedy's.

Let me explain.

Our nation's children and teens are increasingly struggling with anxiety, and I believe at least some of that can be tied to a lack of responsibility. So when Kennedy began facing her own anxiety battles, Gabe and I seized the 4-H opportunity, knowing that seeing her purpose in the caregiving and nurturing of vulnerable animals might fill her with a sense of responsibility. She'd have to work through the daily, mundane activities of feeding and watering these cute little critters and harvesting eggs in order to succeed.

The night we discovered feathers everywhere, Kennedy had failed in one of her responsibilities. It was easy to understand;

the thunderstorm that wreaked havoc an hour earlier coincided with the time she typically locks the chicken coop. But after the storm passed, she'd forgotten.

> **The night we discovered feathers everywhere, Kennedy had failed in one of her responsibilities.**

With tears in her eyes, she said, "I'm sorry. I feel so bad for that chicken." We reassured her, told her this is just how the circle of life goes sometimes.

Weeks later Kennedy bathed the remaining chickens' feet, fluffed their feathers, and entered her five best chickens in the Williamson County Fair. When we arrived that night after the judging was complete, we saw a blue ribbon atop her pen. First prize! Blue-ribbon chickens for Kennedy Lyons!

The responsibility of caring for and protecting those chickens boosted Kennedy's confidence. She knew she'd been given a task, worked hard to carry it out, and succeeded. In the days afterward, I sensed a shift in her demeanor. Anxiousness was giving way to a newfound confidence as she continued to pursue new areas of responsibility in the weeks and months that followed.

What's true for Kennedy is true for all of us. No, we can't work our way out of anxiety or depression (in fact, you can overwork your way into it), but when we are responsible for doing certain things, it makes us feel needed and useful. When we succeed, we're filled with new confidence. If you're stuck in a rut of anxiety, see whether there's some unexplored opportunity for responsibility in your life.

# ❧ Reflect ☙

DO YOU FEEL CAPABLE AND NEEDED IN YOUR LIFE? WHAT ROLE DOES RESPONSIBILITY PLAY IN THOSE FEELINGS? IS THERE A NEW AREA OF RESPONSIBILITY YOU WOULD LIKE TO EXPLORE, AN AREA WHERE YOU FEEL NEEDED?

# 14

# Restoration

You hem me in behind and before,
and you lay your hand upon me.

PSALM 139:5

We'd spent four weeks in quarantine during the COVID-19 pandemic, and I was over the adrenaline rush of a new challenge. We stocked our pantry, had masks and hand sanitizer on standby, and stashed enough toilet paper to last a month. We embraced slower mornings, donned sweatpants with coffee in hand, and mastered the art of working remotely on Zoom. I even tried a dozen new recipes in the kitchen!

The busyness of that first month kept me going, ignoring the dramatic shift I embraced almost subconsciously, overnight. When I lose control, I immediately gravitate to something I can control. But when the scurry fades and the list is checked, I'm left with the feelings I've worked so hard to ignore.

One day I paused long enough to acknowledge to Gabe I felt sad. It felt good to finally own some sort of emotion, prompted from a loss with no end in sight. I was supposed to be teaching in thirty cities in 2020, which ended abruptly on March 8, eight engagements into the year.

I ventured out to the hiking trail adjacent to our home to clear my head. There was still a chill in the air, forlorn trees reluctantly allowing green buds to erupt. The tension was thick; no longer winter, not quite spring. I stopped about two hundred yards down the beaten path, collapsed onto a large rock, and to my surprise, bawled my eyes out. It was the first time I was alone, evidenced by my body's need to release the pressure to keep purposed and positive, with an old-fashioned ugly cry.

For me, crying has always been a cleansing, a laying down of what I cannot control and a release of what I cannot change. I felt almost immediately lighter, more aware of my heart and surroundings. The rest of the hike was more of discovery, taking note of the plant life and critters in the woods not at all affected by a global pandemic. I chuckled at their ignorance of the worry and stress we humans were carrying, nature doing what it does, ready to burst with new life.

I rounded the last turn on the trail, descended back into

my yard, and fell into our hammock. Laying back and gazing at the bright-blue sky, I asked God, "What is the lesson you want me to learn in this season?" And while I don't hear God audibly, without hesitation I felt prompted by a response in my spirit: *You don't have to make things happen.*

Ugh. I'm a firstborn, type A, recovering control freak, one who has been known at times to pride myself on my top two strengths: strategy and responsibility. But those strengths can quickly spiral

> For me, crying has always been a cleansing, a laying down of what I cannot control and a release of what I cannot change.

to weaknesses when I push out of my ability instead of resting in the overflow of God.

One of my favorite quotes by Mother Teresa is in her book *Come Be My Light*, where she says, "When I see someone sad, I always think, she is refusing something to Jesus." I realized I'd been carrying the burden of loss, unwilling to lay it down. I carried grief like a pack on my back, trying every which way to bring life back to the way I left it. But no amount of pantry cleaning would allow me back on a plane, no new recipe would allow me to hug my mother-in-law undergoing her third round of chemo, no Instagram optimism would shake the limits of life on a screen. I needed to lay these burdens down in order to restore peace and gladness in my heart.

# ✄ Reflect ✄

DO YOU LIKE TO MAKE THINGS HAPPEN? IS YOUR BUSYNESS A DESIRE FOR CONTROL IN A LIFE THAT MIGHT FEEL OTHERWISE OVERWHELMING? ASK GOD TO REVEAL WHAT YOU'VE PUSHED INTO YOUR LIST OF RESPONSIBILITIES THAT HE'D LIKE TO RELEASE YOU OF. THIS IS AN INVITATION TO A SLOWER PACE, FULL OF RESPITE AND REDISCOVERY.

# 15

# Being Whole

You discern my going out and my lying
down; you are familiar with all my ways.

PSALM 139:3

When God prompted us to adopt Joy three years ago, it came out of the blue, days before our twenty-year wedding anniversary. For seven years, I'd grown accustomed to being in a different city most weekends from September through May, except for school holiday breaks. I never anticipated this would be the pace of a writer turned teacher. But engagements made way for more in kind, and this new invitation to adopt found me at a crossroads. I'd almost forgotten I had the right to choose.

Desperate for clarity, I begged God aloud, "Does this mean I stop writing?"

A convicting nudge toward my heart responded, *"Do you trust me?"*

I pressed further, "Do I stop traveling?" Again, *"Do you trust me?"*

While this wasn't the answer I was looking for, it was enough to keep going. Through the years, I'd learned that the unexpected call of God always accompanies risk and sacrifice, and I was hungry for it. This would be the third time in my adult life I put all the chips in the middle of the table. First with Cade's diagnosis of Down syndrome in my entrée to motherhood in my twenties, second with leaving home and community in Atlanta to live in New York City in my thirties, and now adding to our family through the gift of a girl on the other side of the world in my forties.

We met Joy on a cloudy December day in China, and fourteen days later we returned home right before Christmas. Healthy attachment for a child who's never experienced a mom or a dad by age five takes three to six months, minimum. She had never experienced any type of family, and as parents we were the only ones who could meet her needs, so I canceled all work plans until she would start school later in the fall.

> **We met Joy on a cloudy December day in China, and fourteen days later we returned home right before Christmas.**

There's something about settling into the decision to stay home. Like riding a bike, I picked up the muscle memory of a decade prior, when I was a mama with three toddlers in tow. I remembered her with empathy, never having enough moments in the day, constantly cooking and cleaning up messes, anxious for nap time. I wanted to return differently, a little older and wiser, with a perspective I couldn't have had then. I wanted to enjoy cooking lessons and bedtime books; nowhere to go, nowhere to be.

Weeks into the slowing of winter, a friend interviewed me for a podcast, curious about this new change of pace and scenery. I almost declined the interview because I couldn't imagine what I'd say, but I gave it a go one day during nap time. Her final question caught me off guard: "When God looks at you right now, what does he think about your season?"

A lump formed in my throat as the tears welled. "For most of my life, I've compartmentalized my roles, but God doesn't. He's restoring the fullness of who I am from my earliest days. Not a fragmented or fractured Rebekah, but a whole coming back together."

When God calls us to be a daughter or mother, to a vocation inside or outside the home, *all these things* work together for good, for those who love God and are called according to his purpose.[1]

Perhaps God wants to change your desires, cramp your style,

show you that his fullness looks different than what you currently see. It's the breadth of the still and quiet moments, without hiding. There's still risk, work, and offering something to the world. In the tension the music is made. This is the fullness God calls us to.

## ❧ Reflect ❧

TAKE A MOMENT. ASK GOD WHAT HE INTENDS FOR YOUR LIFE IN THIS PARTICULAR SEASON. IS THIS A SEASON OF STEPPING OUT, TO RISK IN NEW VENTURES? PERHAPS YOU NEED TO SLOW DOWN AND ENTER THE QUIET RESPITE OF HOME? WHATEVER THE INVITATION, ASK GOD TO MEET YOU IN THE CADENCE, WHETHER GOING OR SLOWING. THESE ARE ALL PLACES GOD DWELLS.

# 16

# Going Against the Grain

Whether you turn to the right or to the
left, your ears will hear a voice behind
you, saying, "This is the way; walk in it."

ISAIAH 30:21

Pierce, our seventeen-year-old, bounded into the living room and declared, "Mom and Dad, I want to homeschool my senior year!" Gabe and I looked at each other, surprised. Before a word could come out of my mouth, my mind raced with the obvious questions:

*Who will be your teacher?*

*How can I take on one more responsibility?*

*It's your senior year, why would you want to miss out on that?*

He's a great kid—handsome, artistic, thoughtful, and kind.

Pierce has always carried the "middle-child" position with grace. Playing lead to an older brother with special needs makes a child grow up quick. Few children could carry the burdensome moments with ease, but Pierce is one of them. His ability to find the positive perspective in any situation is a game changer in our family dynamic.

That is why his counterintuitive drive to switch life up his senior year caught us off guard. Most kids can't wait for their senior experience; football games, dances, trips, and parties are the payoff from years of hard work behind the desk. But as he began to explain, it became clear he was willing to surrender all of that for a vision of something better.

Many of us live day to day in the script we've been provided. Get up, make breakfast, get the kids off to school, go to the gym, grab a bite to eat, go to work, do the laundry, run a few errands, make dinner, watch television, fall in bed exhausted.

But do we feel fulfilled at night?

Are we creating the life we want to live?

Are we living in freedom and with intention?

Christ calls us to follow him into a life of freedom. However, it will feel countercultural. Any decision that goes against the grain will require intention, and it's worth it. Living under the expectations others unknowingly put on us, while trying to people-please, keeps us trapped in a life we may not want.

Conforming to the way others think we should make decisions, schedule our days, and plan for our future is a recipe for disappointment. Instead, we must seek God's best and discern his truest path for our season ahead.

> Christ calls us to follow him into a life of freedom.

Pierce had a vision for his senior year that we couldn't see. He wanted to take back eight hours of his day that were traditionally spent in a school building and turn them with intention to preparing for the call God has in front of him. He saw a vision that would allow him to focus his energy and creativity. He wanted to make music, improve his singing and songwriting skills, all while completing courses from home and dual enrolling in college classes to give him a jump start on his freshman year in college.

As parents, it quickly became clear that this would be a gift, a year of quality time with Pierce before he heads off to college. Our days would be marked by more conversations, workouts, writing sessions, discipleship, and living with intention.

What a year it's been! The growth in Pierce is obvious to all who know him. He's living into a vision that few others could have seen or predicted. He's brimming with confidence from the courage to live with intention. The fruit is clear: he's living a more disciplined life, developing his talents and skills in music, getting ahead in his studies, and having the margin to enjoy relationships. In turn, we're surprised we didn't see the opportunity sooner. I guess there is wisdom in the mouths of babes.

# Reflect

ARE YOU LIVING A LIFE WITH INTENTION OR CONFORMING TO THE EXPECTATIONS OF OTHERS? WHAT WOULD GOING AGAINST THE GRAIN LOOK LIKE IN YOUR SCHEDULE, PRIORITIES, AND COMMITMENTS? ASK GOD TO GIVE YOU A VISION FOR YOUR LIFE BEYOND WHAT OTHERS MIGHT SEE, THEN HAVE THE COURAGE TO STEP INTO IT.

# 17

# Mornings with God

Let me hear of your unfailing love each
morning, for I am trusting you. Show me
where to walk, for I give myself to you.

PSALM 143:8 NLT

E arly mornings are my favorite. It wasn't always this way. For years I rebelled against the six a.m. alarm of my youth. But as a mama of a toddler and teens, I relish these early moments when the house is hushed and reverent.

Each morning, coffee brews, the comforting cadence of hot water dripping through freshly ground beans echoing in the empty kitchen. I light a candle or start a fire, depending on the season. If it's cold, I'll spread a thick blanket in front of the fire and quiet my heart as I kneel in child's pose, arms extended over my head, palms up.

Once here, in God's presence, I feel no urgency to leave, as the prayers flow freely. I ask, listen, and wait. In those moments, God bends low to meet us in our intention. He gives strength to help us push through all the daily chaos and confusion.

My morning routine starts with prayer because it leads me to comfort and shields me from the world's spin cycle of striving, stress, and anxiety. It roots my day in fullness instead of scarcity. When I'm well-rooted, I then turn to my journal.

> My morning routine starts with prayer because it leads me to comfort and shields me from the world's spin cycle of striving, stress, and anxiety.

We all journal in different ways, I suppose, but often, I'll scratch out my ongoing dialogue with God. Each entry begins with the setting, the time, the date. As much as these entries help me discern the direction of any given day, I know they'll serve as reminders of God's faithfulness in the days to come.

After journaling, I turn to God's Word, which nourishes my soul and fills me up after the previous day's pouring out. Through the Scriptures, I learn who he's made me to be, how to live a life that looks more like Christ's, and how to love others well.

Sometimes I take a passage and camp there, or a long section of Psalms, sometimes an entire book at a time in the Old or New Testament. But each day, this time in the Scriptures is like the table set by God in Psalm 23. It's a feast the Father has laid out for me, offering me everything I will need as I set out for the rest of the day.

The last step of my morning routine is gratitude—giving thanks for the things that have already happened, the things that are happening, and the things that will come. Culminating my morning routine with a closing prayer of thanks, I emerge ready to face the day.

God promises to be our comforter and help, but we have to give him an opportunity to do just that. If we don't make space for him, if we don't build it into our routine, how will he meet us where we need him most?

What's your morning routine? Let me encourage you to begin your mornings with God. Meet him with expectation, ready to hear from him. Meet him in prayer, in journaling, in the Scriptures, in gratitude. As you meet him, expect him to bring comfort and strength to your day.

## ❧ Reflect ❧

CONSIDER WHAT YOU WOULD MOST LIKE YOUR MORNING
ROUTINE TO BE. IN WHAT WAYS—PRAYER, JOURNALING, THE
READING OF GOD'S WORD—DO YOU WANT TO MEET WITH GOD?
WHAT STEPS DO YOU NEED TO TAKE TO MAKE THIS MORNING
ROUTINE A REALITY?

# 18

# Pulling Weeds

Each of you should use whatever gift you
have received to serve others, as faithful
stewards of God's grace in its various forms.

1 PETER 4:10

O n my first Saturday home after two weekends of travel, I
woke early. I brewed a pot of coffee and, with steaming
mug in hand, ventured to the rockers on the front porch. Once
seated, I couldn't avoid noticing the weeds taking over the front
and sides of our Tennessee home. Many were taller than me. The
tangled green thicket of undesirables was enough to hide the
flower beds altogether. What was left starving for sunlight under-
neath? I didn't know, but I felt up to the challenge for reasons I

couldn't yet understand. I wanted to get my hands dirty and see tangible results.

So I dove in. I pulled and pulled until my lower back was sore and knees ached from the constant crouching and shuffling. Still, I kept going. Little by little, order returned, and it was beautiful. I was six hours in, and there was no stopping now. I pushed through another two hours. Then three. I barely noticed the setting sun until Gabe pointed it out. After dinner that night, I sank onto my bed, exhausted and grateful. I couldn't wait to get back to it the next morning.

I woke on Sunday at six. In the early morning quiet, as I worked, I remembered telling my friend a couple of weeks prior that I was in the middle of a foundation-shifting season, and the metaphor of clearing the dirt foundation bordering our home was not lost on me. My excitement about working in the yard that weekend was a tangible expression of how I used to feel about my work. In the beginning, I was passionate to write and teach with energy to spare, coming up with new ideas and concepts each day and even into the night. God would press thoughts onto my heart, and I'd jot them down as quickly as they came. But over the years, that passion began to wane. I

> I wanted that endless energy back. I wanted to recover the passion that surrounded my vocation.

wanted that endless energy back. I wanted to recover the passion that surrounded my vocation.

Each of us is made for something specific, given a particular passion by God so we can partner with him in creating and constructing the kingdom.[1] When we discover that passion, when we live into it, we become more alive.

Yet in recent years, I had allowed other things to crowd out my one specific thing, the greatest thing. I said yes to speaking at conferences, even if the topic wasn't a direct fit. I'd spread myself too thin with activities at home as well. Then there was social media. Many distractions overtook the simplicity of the call, and I found myself on the edge of burnout.

So just as I'd pulled weeds in the garden, I pulled the distractions away, one by one. As I cleared space, as I gained margin, my passion was reignited. I began to dive into challenging books. I jotted down new ideas during afternoon walks. I found myself writing and teaching with renewed excitement when I made room again for what I was created to do.

What's choking your passion, your work, the place where your creative energy was meant to go? Pull the weeds. Get them at the root so they don't grow back. Then, with renewed passion, create something beautiful with God.

HAVE YOUR PASSIONS GOTTEN LOST IN THE WEEDS OF DISTRAC-
TION? WHAT THINGS DO YOU NEED TO PRUNE BACK OR PERHAPS
COMPLETELY PULL FROM YOUR LIFE? ASK GOD TO HELP YOU
RECOVER THE PASSION HE PLACED IN YOU.

# Say

# to Yourself

# 19

# Working with Your Hands

Make it your goal to live a quiet
life, minding your own business
and working with your hands.

1 THESSALONIANS 4:11 NLT

I grew up watching my mama sew. She'd bought a repossessed Touch & Sew in 1965 from the Singer store downtown. It was stored in a wooden cabinet, and the whir of this magical machine was the melodic backdrop of my upbringing.

I was ten when I finally received a green light to make my first garment on Mama's sewing machine. I chose a sleeveless blouse with pink and blue stripes (these were my colors because I was a "summer"). I thought a sleeveless pattern would be easiest. Turns out it wasn't. I became quite familiar with terms like *piping* and *interfacing* before the project was complete. At long last, my sewing skills took center stage when I wore this beauty with some culottes to the first day of summer sleepaway camp.

Over the next twenty years, I continued to take on sewing projects. I liked the freedom to create any look I wanted at little cost, and once I'd figured out the building blocks of sewing, the creative process of working with my hands felt almost therapeutic. I learned I could make just about anything with patience, a pattern, and a little attention to detail.

When Gabe and I married, I took to the art of making window treatments like it was my job. This decorating frenzy spiraled into sewing draped end-table covers, pillow shams, and comforters for each bed, and, yes, I even took on

> Once I'd figured out the building blocks of sewing, the creative process of working with my hands felt almost therapeutic.

the daunting task of reupholstering vintage armchairs and an old sofa with a trusty staple gun.

I look back on those years of working with my hands and see how it offered a sense of accomplishment and grew my confidence. What's more, whenever anxiety arose, I could always turn to some creative effort with my hands, and I'd find relief.

Maybe it's just me, but it seems that in this ultra-busy, highly automated, computer-oriented world, we work with our hands less and less. Instead of making clothes, we buy them. Instead of reupholstering our own chairs, we pay someone else to do it. Is it any wonder, then, that we have so much stress and anxiety?

Creating something with your hands (like a sweater, or loaf of bread, or piece of art) won't happen without planning and preparation. You'll need to identify what it is that you want to create (whatever it is, the making of it should be joy filled and non-anxious). Consider exploring an old hobby, like sewing, or trying something new, like calligraphy or watercolor painting.

Once you identify what you want to create, you might need to find a pattern or download a set of instructions or find a DIY video on YouTube. Then, set aside the time to create. Since we have only twenty-four hours every day, this usually means finding a day I can unplug online, which frees up extra time to be fully present and immerse myself in tackling something new without distraction. Creating something from scratch can sometimes feel daunting, but when we're engaged in the act itself, we'll find release from the stress, depression, and anxiety of the world outside.

In other words, using our hands, employing our God-given creativity to make something new, is good medicine for the soul.

# ❧ Reflect ❧

IS THERE SOMETHING CREATIVE YOU'VE BEEN ITCHING TO TRY? GATHER SUPPLIES, PATTERNS, AND PLANS, AND CARVE OUT SOME CREATIVE TIME FOR YOURSELF. DO YOU FIND THAT THE PROCESS OF CREATION—REGARDLESS OF THE RESULT—IS GOOD FOR YOUR SOUL?

# 20

# It's Okay to Say No

"Teach them to your children. Talk about
them when you are at home and when
you are on the road, when you are going
to bed and when you are getting up."

DEUTERONOMY 11:19 NLT

T he feeling of claustrophobia settled in. I was used to occasional episodes of shortness of breath, but never from casually looking at my calendar. This was a new low. A calendar is meant to organize a life, not create panic. Saying yes always sounded wonderful in the moment, until I realized too late what it would take to pull it off. So I found myself scrambling from appointment to obligation in frenetic fashion, running behind with a perpetual feeling of overwhelm. I was desperate for change.

One night I pulled Gabe aside and said, "Something has to give. We have too much going on, and I can't maintain it. We need to stop saying yes, even if it sounds good, and start saying no. The pause will bring the clarity we need. We are starved for quality time and need some new family rhythms."

One extra commitment may seem like a small thing, but as time adds up, our lives begin to spin out of control. Good intentions to show up for meaningful moments, even help our kids succeed and thrive, can go terribly wrong when we are running on fumes. By the weekend, it's easy to look up and feel more disconnected, divided, and disoriented than ever. With no intentional moments of pastoring our children's hearts or creating space for purposeful engagement, everyone can feel a longing we can't describe.

Gabe received my message loud and clear and called a family meeting. Gathered around the fire, we confessed to the kids that quality time was missing in our family and we wanted to change that. They opened up, acknowledging how much they love extended conversations when we take time to ask questions and raise the real dilemmas they face. I reminded them that these conversations happen best in rhythm.

> Good intentions to show up for meaningful moments . . . can go terribly wrong when we are running on fumes.

Creating family rhythms became a priority. We realized connection and belonging begin in the home, so we began the rhythm of embrace, with hugs all around! We got intentional about long dinners, the perfect setting for a captive audience to share about their day—no confrontations, just questions. At bedtime, we got serious about the rhythm of engagement. We tucked Cade and Joy in first with books and songs, then stayed up late for longer conversations with Kennedy and Pierce. We shared responsibilities as "Team Lyons," utilizing a family chore chart on an acrylic board in our kitchen.

Real teamwork happens when everyone has a role. Instead of shortness of breath, I was feeling more relaxed knowing we were taking charge of our time. It seemed counterintuitive, but in saying no, I was saying yes to something better.

# ❧ Reflect ❧

DO YOU FEEL OVERWHELMED BY ALL OF THE COMMITMENTS
IN YOUR HOME? WHICH ONES ARE DRAINING YOU, AND WHICH
ONES ARE BRINGING LIFE? LOOK AT YOUR CALENDAR FOR THE
NEXT SEVEN DAYS. IDENTIFY THREE TASKS THAT YOU CAN SAY
NO TO THIS WEEK. LOOK FOR THINGS THAT DON'T CONTRIBUTE
TO YOUR FAMILY'S IDENTIFIED PRIORITIES, AND REMOVE THEM
FROM YOUR LIST. TAKE THAT TIME TO SAY YES TO THE THINGS
THAT ACTIVELY RESTORE YOU.

# 21

# Expressing Your Emotions

"Blessed are those who mourn,
for they will be comforted."

MATTHEW 5:4

On February 1, 2001, I was thirty-nine weeks pregnant. I waddled into my obstetrician's office for a final, routine checkup. But there was nothing routine in the events of the next few hours. Two ultrasounds, two epidurals, and a C-section later, Cade Christian Lyons was born into this world.

Six hours later, at one a.m., I was still sleeping off the meds when the door opened and a doctor spoke from the threshold, telling us he saw signs of Down syndrome. A geneticist would run tests to be certain.

For five days I held out hope. When at last the phone rang,

and I heard Gabe answer, I knew it was the doctor calling with the lab results. Seeing the look on his face, I collapsed.

There will never be words to describe the pain I felt at that moment. I had no idea I was capable of such grief, yet there I was, wailing. I could not shed the anguish fast enough.

Something died in me that day: the controlled plan for my "perfect" life. In return, something was born that day: surrender to an uncharted and forever-changing path. As my body slowly emptied of tears, I noticed something. I was weeping in both body and spirit, my body trembling beyond control, yet a transfer was happening. Jesus was taking my pain on himself. He'd done the same on the cross, for all of us.

We walked into the NICU, and as I swept up Cade in my arms, his eyes made contact with mine as if to say, "Will you love me for me? Not for what I can do or accomplish? Not for the milestones I can meet so you feel like a good mom?"

The performer in me melted. Already those sky-blue eyes were reminding me that God doesn't measure worth in terms of ability but in terms of identity. We're sons and daughters, adopted into the family of God, grafted onto the vine of Jesus, heirs to a throne. My grief, just a few hours old, was already bringing me comfort.

> God doesn't measure worth in terms of ability but in terms of identity.

Some people believe the Christian life makes no room for sadness, gives no permission for grief, allows no time for lament. This kind of mental toughness might seem like the best approach for immediate survival, but unexpressed grief can become a bitterness that chokes us.

*If we cannot grieve, we cannot be comforted.*[1]

Jesus never lacked emotion or expression. He wept with his dear friends Mary and Martha when their brother, Lazarus, died.[2] He also wept loudly for the fate of his beloved Jerusalem.[3] And when he was in the garden that final evening before he was arrested, Jesus wept for himself.[4] Jesus mourned, and when he was finished mourning, he surrendered to the work of God—work that brought great freedom to all of us.

Every time we express grief, we allow Jesus to absorb our pain. When we live out the freedom we have been given to grieve, Jesus takes our grief on himself and replaces it with comfort. What a precious gift.

# Reflect

DO YOU ALLOW TEARS TO FALL AND GRIEF TO BE FULLY EX-PRESSED? OR DO YOU STUFF AWAY, RUNNING AWAY FROM THE SORROW? HOW MIGHT CHRIST'S COMFORT LIE ON THE OTHER SIDE OF GRIEVING? ASK GOD TO STEP INTO YOUR GRIEF, TO HELP YOU EXPRESS IT, AND TO COMFORT YOU AS ONLY HE CAN.

# 22

## Strength in Weakness

Cast all your anxiety on him
because he cares for you.

1 PETER 5:7

I can't explain why fear is so pervasive in our society. I can
only speak to the ways my own fear unraveled me and how
God was faithful, even in the dark. My panic stemmed from the
persistent trauma and physical exhaustion related to caring for
a highly unpredictable, special-needs child. But even though my
anxiety was justifiable, that did not negate the damaging impact
it had on my soul.

Most of us carry chronic stress for so long we no longer
recognize the weight of it. That's why I call it a grace when our
bodies rebel. It is God's way of saying, "No more."

How many of us try to manage our stress with some method of numbing ourselves? The problem with pain management is exactly that: we are *managing*. What if we are called to acknowledge our pain, to confess our inability to beat it? What if we're called to admit our weakness and declare that only God's strength is sufficient?

God wants us to reveal our weakness—to recognize what traumatizes and exhausts us. He wants us to confess our wounds, our sources of pain and stress, and bring them into the light so he can redeem and transform them with his strength.

I'm often asked, "When you were in the thick of panic attacks and depression, did you ever feel disqualified from ministering to others?" During that season, I wrestled silently. Perhaps I was afraid that if I acknowledged my weakness, others would think my faith was small. But these days, I proactively confess my weakness and my continuing need for God's help in my fight against panic. On a weekly basis I press in, ask him to show me anything I'm not seeing.

The need for self-examination never ends. Paul told us, "Everyone ought to examine themselves before they eat of the bread and drink from the cup."[1] If we do not, he wrote, we become sick and weak, bringing judgment on ourselves.[2] Heart examinations are powerful. I wrestle with my own in the early hours, through prayers and writing in my journal.

God delights in us. He doesn't want us to live in bondage. When we invite him into our places of weakness, he comes and says, "Let's nail this thing. Let's not dance around it, perform around it, or seek validation to make it feel better. Let's just go after it."

> **God delights in us. He doesn't want us to live in bondage.**

This kind of healing could bring you into one of your richest seasons, but make no mistake about it: when you confess that God is the strength in your weakness, things may seem worse for a time. Why? Because when you find yourself on the cusp of strongholds being released, the enemy marches in double time.

This is why it is critical to keep declaring the truth: God has promised that when we are dependent on him, he walks with us. We can ask whatever we will, and he will lavish us with his power, his goodness, his grace, his kindness, and his mercy. He doesn't want to keep us where we are. When we are brave enough to ask him to meet us in our weakness, he comes.

# ⊰⊱ Reflect ⊰⊱

ARE YOU LIVING WITH EXHAUSTION, FEAR, STRESS? WHAT KEEPS
YOU FROM CONFESSING YOUR WEAKNESS, EVEN TO GOD?
HOW MIGHT CONFESSING YOUR NEED FOR GOD'S STRENGTH
INVITE HIS POWER TO WORK IN YOUR LIFE? SPEND SOME TIME
JOURNALING YOUR CONFESSIONS TO GOD.

# 23

# Rhythms of Sleep

In peace I will lie down and sleep, for you
alone, Lord, make me dwell in safety.

PSALM 4:8

I never was a night owl, at least not until my first pregnancy at the age of twenty-five. Then as babies two and three came, I slept even less. Five years into parenthood, I realized my body was programmed to wake every night around three a.m., even if the children didn't wake me.

Some nights I'd wake to use the bathroom and drift back to sleep. Other nights, my mind would rush to what I didn't accomplish the day prior, and I'd create a mental task list. Sometimes I woke with conviction, mulling over how I could have treated someone differently, replaying the conversation in my mind. On rare occasions, I'd pull way out and take a broader inventory, examining and questioning the current season: *Was I living well? Loving well? Focused on what matters?* These racing questions seemed of utmost importance in those pre-dawn hours.

I accepted my new normal, sleeping only half the night, and even though I was always exhausted, I learned how to navigate my life at 60 percent. With an extra shot of caffeine midafternoon and half a Tylenol PM in the evening, I could rally and make my lack of sleep work.

> I accepted my new normal, sleeping only half the night.

But because I wasn't getting enough rest, everything felt overwhelming, and my relationships with those I loved most began to suffer. That's when I knew: it was time to get serious about sleep.

In her book *The Sleep Revolution*, Arianna Huffington reported that we're often unaware of the simple factors contributing to our lack of rest.[1] I began implementing some of her suggestions for creating an environment for better sleep. I started turning down the lights at the end of the evening. I kept devices away from the bed and set the bedroom temperature below seventy degrees. I began taking baths before bed. I even wrote down things I needed to do so I wouldn't wake with a mental list hours later. Those things seemed to help, but it was only the beginning.

I also created a consistent structure for organizing my time each day. I spent the morning hours doing creative work and held meetings over lunch. In the afternoon, I tended to correspondence and then took a brisk walk. As I became more intentional about the rhythm of my days, I fell into bed, content with a day spent well.

I started eating better and walking no less than ten thousand steps a day. The more I slept, the more energy I had to keep this new cycle going. As I caught up on years of missed sleep and reset my rhythms, I became more productive. My fuse was not as short, and I could sense the anxiety, stress, and chaos of my internal world melting away.

Does low-grade anxiety or depression follow you everywhere you go? Are you often distracted? Do you lose it daily? Dig a little. Ask yourself, *Am I getting enough sleep?* If you're not getting between seven and nine hours, change up your rhythms and routines, and make sleep a priority. It'll make all the difference.

# ❧ Reflect ❧

ARE YOU GETTING ENOUGH SLEEP? WHAT CHANGES CAN YOU
MAKE TO THE DAILY RHYTHMS OF YOUR LIFE SO THAT YOU CAN
SLEEP? CRAFT A PLAN FOR BOTH DAYS AND EVENINGS THAT
WILL ENCOURAGE A FULL AND PEACEFUL NIGHT OF REST.

# 24

# A Little Sweat

She sets about her work vigorously;
her arms are strong for her tasks.

PROVERBS 31:17

My first experience of exercise as a stress reliever was in high school. One particular day, in the middle of a mess of stress, I felt like I just needed to run. Maybe it was the pressure of constant band competitions, a rigorous practice schedule, or the general feeling of being overwhelmed, but for whatever reason, running seemed the only option. So I ran. And in the exercise, I found release. After that experience, I kept running—and running and running (which I hope you heard in my best Forrest Gump voice).

In college, I ran the "roller coaster"—a two-mile track of hills that would make any stomach turn. When I moved off campus for my last two years, my roommate ran cross-country, inspiring me to go on longer runs. I ran a regular four-mile loop every morning in our town's historic district, then pushed myself toward an occasional thirteen-mile run. Those long runs provided me with time to think and pray through issues and problems. You can solve a lot of problems during a half marathon!

The summer after my college graduation, I began to run trails. A couple of months in, I tripped on a tree root sticking out of the ground and twisted my knee. Without health insurance and with no money for surgery, I came to the realization that I'd have to heal on my own. My knee pain receded, but I found I could no longer run distances beyond 5K or the pain would return.

I knew I couldn't let my exercise routine go. And even though I picked up spin classes, weight training, and yoga, nothing compares to exercising outdoors. The fresh air, salty sweat, and rush of endorphins bring a calming clarity, even in my most stressful seasons.

Science has long shown how exercise supports mental health by reducing anxiety and depression and by improving self-esteem and cognitive function.[1] Even just five minutes of outdoor activity—like hiking, jogging, or outdoor yoga—can change mood and self-esteem.[2] This isn't new information. But sometimes we lose sight of the most obvious practices when anxiety, panic, or depression hits. Instead of turning to the things God created to bring us some natural positive mojo, we look for comfort foods, nestled on a couch or hidden behind a screen, all of which are sedentary. All of which strip us of both internal and external strength.

**Even just five minutes of outdoor activity . . . can change mood and self-esteem.**

At some point, we have to make a decision and commit. And while it can sometimes be overwhelming to focus on a long-term exercise routine, remember: a routine is just a series of days strung together. So choose to make this day count. Don't end your day if you haven't moved your body in an intentional way. God designed you to break a sweat. Your body, your brain, and your spirit will thank you for it.

## Reflect

WHAT ACTIVITIES, AS WELL AS EXERCISES, DO YOU ENJOY?
HOW CAN YOU INCORPORATE ACTIVITY AND EXERCISE INTO
YOUR EVERYDAY ROUTINE? THINK BEYOND THE TRADITIONAL.
AN AFTERNOON STROLL, A MORNING IN THE GARDEN, OR A
PLAYGROUND ROMP WITH THE KIDS ARE ALL WONDERFUL WAYS
TO EXERCISE. IS IT TIME TO RENEW YOUR GYM MEMBERSHIP OR
START AN ONLINE SERVICE? WHO IS A SAFE PERSON IN YOUR
LIFE WHO CAN HOLD YOU ACCOUNTABLE? MAKE SMALL GOALS.
START AT TEN MINUTES A DAY AND GO FROM THERE.

# 25

## Confession for Your Soul

If we confess our sins, he is faithful and
just and will forgive us our sins and
purify us from all unrighteousness.

1 JOHN 1:9

Please, God, heal my heart."

The prayer surfaced without warning, and once I spoke the words, there was no turning back. A dam broke, releasing tears that had been bottled up for decades. These five words surged repeatedly in rhythm as I knelt on the cold shower floor, tears mingling with the water streaming from above.

I should have seen the signs leading to this moment. I'd wrapped up a week of teaching in California and stumbled back to my room for pj's and comfort food. As I was inhaling a post-speaking-event cheeseburger in a darkened hotel room, I began to watch a talk online by Ann Voskamp.[1] Ten minutes in, the Spirit spoke truth to my heart, and I sat bolt upright in bed.

Quoting Augustine, Ann spoke these words: "You have made us for yourself, O Lord, and our heart is restless until it rests in you." I'd had a restless, striving heart for as long as I could remember.

Ann continued, "Those who keep score in life just want to know that they count. When you work for an audience of One, you always know that you count." Was I restless and anxious because I hadn't learned to serve this singular audience? Was I keeping score?

As I reflected on these questions, I awakened to the truth. I was still striving. After a speaking engagement, I'd second-guess my delivery, or worse, check the number of retweets on Twitter, likes on Facebook, or hearts in my Instagram feed. When the numbers spiked, I spiked. When they dipped, I dipped.

I'd awakened to my calling, but I still wasn't free, I still wasn't whole. I realized the humiliating truth: I was *desperate* for public affection. I kept probing, half asking God, half asking myself: *Do I count? Do I matter?* Then I finally heard God's voice again:

"You matter to me; is that enough?"

> I realized the humiliating truth: I was *desperate* for public affection.

Silence.

"For some reason I'm not doing this for an audience of one," I admitted.

"So I'm not enough?"

"Yeah; you are kind of not enough. Why is this the case?"

I heard the truth in my own spirit: I didn't believe God's love was enough. Instead, I looked to the size and response of my readers in order to feel loved. I relapsed into the performing ways of my past. "Please, God, heal my heart."

The words landed with weighted hope.

Many of us are not free because we have not confessed the sins that hold us captive. *Confession is the gateway to healing, the route to freedom.* What is confession? Confession means "[admitting] you have done something wrong, or [admitting] unwillingly that something is true."[2]

We could start with this simple prayer: "God, I'm sorry I don't live as if you are enough. I'm sorry I substitute achievement, or body image, or food, or sex, or anything for the freedom you bring."

I'd spent years trying to put a Band-Aid on my pain, but only the one who created me, who fashioned and formed me, could revive my broken heart. And he's the only one who can revive yours.

# ❧ Reflect ☙

# 26

# The Renewal of Sabbath

"Come to me, all you who are weary and
burdened, and I will give you rest."

MATTHEW 11:28

We must Sabbath. This practice is essential for our ability to grow in mental, emotional, and spiritual health. We cannot run if we cannot rest.

Taking a rest isn't a sign of weakness. Yet our culture whispers the opposite: if we try harder, work smarter, get that next degree, connect with influencers, and go for our dreams, we just might live a life of significance. But God declares we are *already* chosen, beloved, appointed, and set apart. He ordered our lives with purpose and intention. We don't need to hustle to prove something God says is already true.

Your value as a human being isn't found in *what you produce*; it's found in *who you are in Christ*—a person designed in the image of God to glorify him forever. From the beginning, God designed his creation to be more abundant, fulfilled, and joyful when we work from a place of rest and renewal. When we intentionally Sabbath—stop striving so much—we create space for healing, wholeness, and refreshment.

And the practice of Sabbath doesn't need to be restricted to just a weekly rhythm. You can develop a plan for a quarterly and annual practice as well. These patterns of pause help ensure your life, family, and relationships are receiving the life-giving benefits of uninterrupted time.

> When we intentionally Sabbath—stop striving so much—we create space for healing, wholeness, and refreshment.

Here's how Gabe and I try to do this:

Each week we take time over breakfast or lunch to stop the work and focus on our relationship. Every once in a while, we have an extended date night. We also make sure to have at least one "family night" planned on the weekend, usually a late afternoon and evening dedicated to just the six of us.

Quarterly, we make time for the two of us to take a full day away. And annually, we try to get away for a few days or a long weekend to take time just for us. His parents helped make this possible when the kids were young, and now we try to schedule our getaway while our kids are at summer camp. These days are magic for us. Our conversations go deeper than we seem to ever get in the bustle of life. We get beneath the surface and to the interiors of our hearts.

We also have an annual Sabbath rhythm for our entire family. During December and July, we put aside work travel and intentionally spend time together as a family. We might take an overnight trip somewhere a couple of hours away or a family vacation. Most of the time we stay local and schedule consistent nights and weekends of hikes, concerts, bike rides, ball games, mini golf, movies, and, of course, a progressive tour of Nashville's favorite eats. By building this rhythm into our annual calendar, we stay grounded in a plan that gives life to each member of our family.

This practice of Sabbath rest is often neglected in this harried age. Yet if you want to maintain your emotional, physical, and spiritual health, it's important to reconnect with yourself, God, your family, and your community. Sabbath allows us the space we need to understand our lives are not rooted in work, productivity, or acquisition. Our worth is found in the God who loves us, who created rest for our good.

## ✽✽ Reflect ✽✽

WHAT MOMENTS AND TIMES OF SABBATH DO YOU LONG TO INCLUDE IN YOUR LIFE? TAKE SOME TIME NOW TO MAP OUT THOSE TIMES OF REST AND RENEWAL, BOTH FOR YOURSELF AND YOUR FAMILY. AND THEN, TAKE A TIME OF SABBATH. START WITH A FEW MINUTES AT A TIME, AND WORK UP TO A FULL DAY IF POSSIBLE. YOU'LL FIND YOURSELF EXPERIENCING MORE CLOSENESS WITH GOD AND YOUR LOVED ONES.

# 27

# Taking a Walk

My feet have closely followed his steps; I
have kept to his way without turning aside.

JOB 23:11

It was the third Monday in January 2005, a dull, gray morning in the suburbs of Atlanta. I opened my laptop to look up a term I'd heard on the radio: "seasonal affective disorder." According to the internet, this diagnosis (often known as SAD) is a type of depression that comes and goes with the seasons, typically starting in the late fall or early winter and going away during the spring and summer.[1]

One article led to the next, and I discovered SAD is often the worst on "Blue Monday," a day falling about one month after Christmas and often coined the "most depressing day of the year." Looking back, I could see how I'd been through a few Blue Mondays of my own, though I hadn't realized it.

A few months after that Blue Monday, we moved to New York City, and my primary mode of transportation shifted from the car to my legs. And just a month into that dreaded first winter in New York, I found myself walking outside to the gym in eleven-degree weather, surprised by the spring in my step. There was something nice about the brisk air against my cheeks. *Maybe it wasn't the winter that brought the sadness. Maybe it was my suburban inactivity.* Our life in New York didn't allow for that. I had to use my actual legs and burn some energy.

If I had a meeting? I had to walk.

If I wanted to go to the grocery store? I had to walk.

> I had to use my actual legs and burn some energy.

Pick up the kids from school? Walk.

Even in the dead of winter, those walks lifted my spirits. Creative ideas emerged. I jotted down unexpected thoughts on my phone. I didn't experience any hint of seasonal affective disorder that winter, or during any winter since. I was learning something profound. Walking improved my mental and emotional health.

The average person now spends 9.3 hours sitting per day—far more than the 7.7 hours we spend sleeping.[2] Not only does the lack of exercise make us more susceptible to heart disease, type 2 diabetes, and other ailments that come from a lethargic lifestyle, but it's shutting down our brains and limiting our growth.

After we moved to Tennessee, one of my greatest concerns was how it was going to affect my walking pattern. If I didn't want to settle back into the suburban temptations of comfort and conformed lethargy, I'd need to be strategic.

So Gabe and I made a plan. Daily, we'd get out as a family for evening walks. I'd hike the trails of Lake Radnor with girlfriends or walk the dogs in our neighborhood while Cade rode his bike. Whenever I could, I'd take the stairs. As my step count increased, my productivity increased too.

If walking isn't a part of your daily routine, you're missing out on a key rhythm of restoration, one that can pull you from the doldrums, bring new insights, and kickstart your creativity.

# Reflect

HOW CAN YOU ADD WALKING INTO THE NATURAL, DAILY
RHYTHMS OF YOUR LIFE? CHALLENGE YOURSELF TO TAKE A
LONG WALK THIS WEEK AND DO A LITTLE BRAINSTORMING. BE
SURE TO JOT DOWN ALL THE NEW THOUGHTS YOU THINK.

# 28

# Room to Breathe

"Come with me by yourselves to a
quiet place and get some rest."

MARK 6:31

It was a cool, bright winter day, the kind where the sun is bent on breaking around the branches of every oak and poplar. The warmth of my leather gloves would be necessary on this crisp morning for the work set before us. Our home is bordered by woods, lots of woods.

Growing up a Florida girl near the Gulf of Mexico, I could ride my bike ten minutes to the beach. The expanse of ocean from an endless horizon revealed a craving in my soul. This was my hiding place, a wide-open space. While I love a wooded hike through a tunnel of green, I still need vision. Perhaps it's because

I'm a context junkie and need to understand what's around the bend. Since our home is situated in a wooded hollow, I started to feel closed in each time I looked from our bedroom to a wall of green. Maybe it's my need for white space or a hankering for design—I like order. Gangly trees busting through every space doesn't fit the look.

Today was our day to start clearing. Any tree smaller than a few inches had to go. Chainsaw roaring, brush cutter brimming, Gabe, Pierce, and I began to take dominion and bring order to our woods. Gabe cut branches as high as he could reach, to clear visibility and show off their riddled trunks. Pierce stacked wood for future kindling, and I ran the wood chipper to create mulch. The harmony of engines was music to my ears. Everything had a purpose. Hours later we looked up and discovered the entire landscape had changed. I could see farther and breathe a little easier. Nature needs space to breathe too, but someone has to make room.

In the clutter of our everyday lives, every ounce of margin can be consumed by the next urgent need. The noise and needs never seem to stop—from crying children to a buzzing phone, a sick husband, a leaking roof, or oil-change alerts. These demands force our heads down as we push through our everyday tasks. But this is the opposite of what our souls need.

Life in Christ calls us to stop, make room, and rest. Mark

6:31 captures a curious moment when Jesus decided to make room. People kept coming and going, keeping him and the disciples so busy they didn't have a chance to eat. Jesus stopped and said to his friends, "Come with me by yourselves to a quiet place and get some rest."

Just as Jesus practiced his rhythm of going to the hills to pray before embarking on ministry, he wanted them to experience the same. He understood the need for input from the Father before having anything to offer to those in need. By making room and creating space, he and the disciples would have more to give.

> Life in Christ calls us to stop, make room, and rest.

The oak grows best when it has space. In the same way, we must make room for our souls to breathe. A cluttered life leads to disordered living—and there is too much at stake to run our lives on empty. Likewise, we need space to take in the necessary nutrients and light that allow us to flourish. When roots go deep without competition, the strength they build is incomprehensible. Clear away the clutter. Delete some appointments and activities from the to-do list. Fight the fear of missing out and make room for yourself.

The next morning after we cleared, Gabe and I sat on our front porch, coffees in hand, admiring a magnificent sunrise we couldn't see prior. I laughed with delight. Who knew rolling hills could mirror the expanse of the ocean? We looked at each other and grinned at my vision. Clearing the clutter helped me exhale and made room for light to break through.

## ⤷ Reflect ⤶

IS YOUR SETTING ONE OF ORDER OR OF CLUTTER? DO YOU FEEL
THE STRAIN OF TOO MUCH ACTIVITY IN YOUR LIFE? AS YOU LOOK
AT THE WEEK AHEAD, INVITE GOD INTO YOUR CIRCUMSTANCES
AND BE INTENTIONAL TO MAKE ROOM FOR THE PRIORITIES THAT
WILL HELP YOU BREATHE.

# 29

# Seasons of Rest

It is by grace you have been saved,
through faith—and this is not from
yourselves, it is the gift of God—not
by works, so that no one can boast.

EPHESIANS 2:8–9

When we moved to Franklin, Tennessee, from New York City, I began hearing a refrain. Friends would comment in passing or look me square in the eye and say, *"You are entering a season of rest."* But I did not want to rest.

There was work to be done—people to minister to, friends to encourage, loved ones to set free! *Rest is not something a runner wants to hear about.* Leaving behind the fast pace of the city, I felt like I'd been benched or, worse, tripped in my lane while the rest of the runners went whizzing by.

During this period my lifelong friend Trina came to visit. She brought me *Abide in Christ* by Andrew Murray, a consequential book written in 1895. It was a timely love letter on the relationship between the Vine (Jesus) and the branch (the believer). Between sips of coffee and blueberry scones, I devoured it.

I wouldn't have asked for it, but the Lord awakened me at four a.m. every day for four weeks straight so I could read. I savored every page; it became dog-eared, the text inside underlined, circled, and highlighted, with exclamation points filling the margins. As I studied, I wrote my own nuggets of truth and wisdom in my journal. As the winter unfolded, one message rang loud and clear:

> **In the quiet I heard God whisper... "I need you to take a rest."**

*Stop performing for love.*

Why was I still struggling to let go of this particular stronghold and to walk in freedom? Somewhere deep down, I still believed you had to "Put your head down and work hard! There's a harvest, go get it!"

In the quiet I heard God whisper the opposite: "I need you to take a rest."

In other words, I didn't need to work harder or fight more. I didn't need to hustle or strive.

I released my plans for serving him and took the vow to initiate nothing. I would rest. I would wait to see what he unfolded.

When I stopped running, Jesus drew near. And I learned something, something I'll hold tightly forever: *God cares more about our presence than our performance.*

I'd always thought my closeness with Jesus was dependent on me. Consequently, I was an Energizer Bunny for him. But Jesus' love draws us in for one thing: to come into his presence and his rest, to stop working and doing and striving, to remain in him. That's it.

God chooses us, and we choose him. God blesses us, and we bless him. But this exchange cannot happen unless we first learn to rest and abide in him. If we are not free to rest, we will either burn out or the work will be about our agenda, not God's. He wants us to stop trying so hard to matter.

What a beautiful relief! The old covenant was about what we brought to *him*: our annual offering, our covering of sin to become restored with God. The new covenant is all about what Jesus brings to *us*: his offering, his blood to forgive our sins, and his righteousness credited to us, making us right with God.

God's got this. He's done the work, and we are free to rest.

## ❧ Reflect ❧

DO YOU BELIEVE GOD CARES MORE ABOUT YOUR PRESENCE
THAN YOUR PERFORMANCE? OR DO YOU FEEL PRESSURED TO
KEEP RUNNING, TO "EARN" YOUR PLACE WITH GOD? WHAT IF
YOU CHOSE TO SIMPLY REST IN HIS PRESENCE?

# 30

## Something New

"Come," [Jesus] said.
Then Peter got down out of the boat, walked
on the water and came toward Jesus.

MATTHEW 14:29

There was too much chaos, too much stuff. Too many piles. The truth was, the stacks had been building for years, but I'd always found excuses to avoid them. But all my excuses finally caught up with me.

It began with the simple practice of noticing. I noticed all the piles. Piles in the laundry room and on the kitchen island. Stacks of books by the bedside. A closet full of clothes I hadn't worn for years. Though my house wasn't dirty—dishes cleaned, floors vacuumed, and unpiled places dusted—the piles and stacks remained like survivors weathering a storm.

I'm sure this sounds silly to those of you who are natural organizers, but I find organization difficult. To make matters worse, I so often stuff my schedule full of commitments that the last thing I want to do in my downtime is tend to the chronic chaos. But with new inspiration, I determined to push myself to create a serene family space.

I read articles, watched online videos, and scoured Pinterest for ideas. I flipped through books about tidiness and decluttering and formulated a plan.

I'd go through the piles room by room and create a place for everything in our home. I'd keep what I needed, donate or sell the things I didn't, and encourage Gabe and the kids to do the same.

For weeks I pushed myself. As the chaos of each room gave way to order, I noticed a sort of peace setting in as well as a sense of pride and accomplishment. And after months of work, the results were evident. My home was put together—and it was calm. So was my interior life. Pushing myself led to tangible, healthier results.

In recent years, I've found unexpected joy in pushing myself, and not just organizationally. I've pushed myself athletically, in my writing life, and as a mother, learning to listen and give my children what they need. When we push ourselves, we discover how much we can accomplish, how brave we can be, and how strong we really are.

Pushing ourselves helps break the monotony of an otherwise mundane routine. Don't you get tired of making the same coffee, packing the same lunches, and paying the same bills? I know I do. But when we break up the routine, when we try new things and create opportunities for different feelings to emerge, we grow, and we change the dynamic.

> When we push ourselves, we discover how much we can accomplish, how brave we can be, and how strong we really are.

You might be asking, *What happens if I try something new, if I push myself and fail?* That's okay. Even when we fail, we learn new things. We might learn different ways to attack a challenge or discover that an activity is not for us. Anytime we venture into new territory, we are likely to experience setbacks. But when we push through, we find it's okay to try new things, no matter the outcome.

So what might you do to push yourself? Could you try some new activity, take on a new hobby, or even learn a new language? Push yourself and have fun with it. See whether a little hard work and a little success don't make a difference in your emotional and mental outlook.

# ᴙᴙ Reflect ᴙᴙ

IS THERE SOMETHING NEW YOU'VE BEEN WANTING TO TRY, TO
TACKLE, OR TO DO—SOMETHING THAT SEEMS OVERWHELMING
OR OUTSIDE YOUR COMFORT ZONE? MAYBE YOU'VE WANTED TO
TRY TENNIS, WRITE YOUR NOVEL, OR REACH OUT TO SOMEONE
IN YOUR FIELD FOR A NETWORKING COFFEE. WHAT IS HOLDING
YOU BACK? RESOLVE TO DO ONE THING OUTSIDE YOUR
COMFORT ZONE THIS WEEK, AND NO MATTER WHAT HAPPENS,
REJOICE KNOWING YOU'RE LIVING THIS ONE LIFE YOU HAVE.

# 31

# Dreaming Dreams

For we are God's handiwork, created in
Christ Jesus to do good works, which
God prepared in advance for us to do.

EPHESIANS 2:10

I love books by dead people. So much of their prose cuts through the noisy clichés of today. I inhaled *Man's Search for Meaning* a few years ago as we traveled through the Irish countryside, through forests and castles and sheep. As I read, I stumbled across Viktor Frankl's words about himself: "The meaning of your life is to help others find the meaning of theirs."[1] I read the sentence again, then burst into happy tears. "That's what I want!"

Frankl's premise was that anxiety flows from a life without meaning and purpose. When we lose meaning, we live with a sense of unfulfilled responsibility, rooted in anxiety. With meaning, though, we're free of anxiety. Through freedom, we're given a great responsibility.

As compelling as Frankl's words were, I knew they were an echo of Scripture. Paul wrote, "Just make sure that you don't use this freedom as an excuse to do whatever you want to do and destroy your freedom. Rather, use your freedom to serve one another in love; that's how freedom grows."[2]

The freedom we've been given by our Creator has been coupled with the responsibility to serve humanity. When we abdicate this responsibility, our freedom is purposeless. In the landscape of today, many people—women in particular—don't realize the purpose and value they bring to the world. Whether it's because of family norms, traditional understandings of gender roles, or societal pressure, women have grown used to conforming to a shadow of who they were designed to be. And we wonder why so many women struggle with anxiety, stress, and depression.

> The freedom we've been given by our Creator has been coupled with the responsibility to serve humanity.

How do you find your purpose, your values, your own dreams? Grab a pen and a piece of paper. Sit in the silence and dream. Picture the future you want for yourself, your marriage, your kids. Ask yourself: *Who am I meant to be? What am I meant to do?*

Then, of course, there's the question of time. As I travel the country and speak with women of all ages, women who've been relegated to the sidelines as they've tended to children or served in administrative positions, or were minimized in their influence, are asking questions like, *How do I imagine a life of purpose when there seems to be so little time?*

For us, Gabe and I look for active ways to support each other in the callings God puts on our lives. We share the responsibilities of managing a household and nurturing our kids' hearts. And if one of us has a dream that's important, that's worth chasing, the other helps make that happen.

I recognize every relational circumstance looks different. You have unique obstacles to living out your dreams. But with a little imagination, a little nurturing of the dream, a little collaboration with your spouse, children, or friends, you just might find a path through those obstacles.

We were designed to dream and to take responsibility for those dreams. And when we tap into our dreams, when we walk forward in them, God gives us renewed meaning and a purpose for our lives.

## ✒ Reflect ✒

DO YOU KNOW YOUR DREAMS? IF SO, WRITE THEM HERE, ALONG WITH THE NEXT STEP YOU CAN TAKE TO FURTHER THOSE DREAMS. IF YOU'RE NOT SURE OF YOUR DREAMS, CARVE OUT SOME TIME TO STEP AWAY, TO GRAB PAPER AND PEN, AND TO ASK: WHAT DREAMS WOULD I LIKE TO PURSUE? HOW DO THEY INTERSECT WITH GOD'S PURPOSE FOR MY LIFE?

# 32

# Healthy Play

The joy of the Lord is your strength.

NEHEMIAH 8:10

I'd just finished my fourteenth trip in less than twelve weeks, and there were still two left before the holidays. But before those last two events, Gabe and I would have a break, a gathering with dear friends on a ranch in Sedalia, Colorado, and boy, did I need it. I was ready to be free of it all, to have some fun.

We met the wrangler at the barn and soon were headed out on the trail. The autumn air was crisp, the sky bright blue as we practiced the basics of steer, walk, and post a trot over and over in a wide-open field. As I grew more comfortable on the back of my horse, my excitement grew.

The wrangler then decided I was ready to try out a lope,

a full-on run the likes of which you'd see in a Western movie. Despite my protests, he wouldn't let me off the hook: "Trust me, you'll love it," he said.

Love it? Yeah, right.

As we picked up the pace, I felt out of control, which is the *worst* feeling for a not-yet-recovered control freak. Almost falling off the side of the horse, I yelled, "Stop!" Unlike trotting, which requires you to *do* something, the guide told me that when loping, I needed to allow the horse to carry the responsibility while I relaxed in the saddle. I nodded, still uneasy. Just before the horse took off the second time, I whispered a prayer: "God, please remove all fear today. I want to enjoy your creation, as a daughter, wild and free. Replace the fear with joy!"

The horse picked up speed, and as I relaxed into the three-beat cadences, my right arm flung out wide like a rodeo girl. The wind blew through my hair. The sunlight was warm on my cheeks, and I was smiling. A smile? Wow! It was in that realization that I began gut laughing. Full-on, joyful laughter. I'd given over my need to control and was able to experience the beauty of this wild animal running free. It was exhilarating! It was freedom!

> **The horse picked up speed, and as I relaxed into the three-beat cadences, my right arm flung out wide like a rodeo girl.**

If this was what playing feels like, I'd like more. The ride swept me back to my childhood, before the need for control took over, before I learned to be afraid. When I had no shortage of confidence or imagination. When I invited bite-size acts of courage into everyday play.

As I've reflected on my experience at the ranch, I've come to realize this: play and control cannot coexist. Afraid of taking a risk, of losing control, I often miss opportunities for play, which is a shame because it's play that breaks us out of our stressful routines and rejuvenates us. It's play that so often restores our freedom and joy. And it's play that shows us that everything won't fall apart when we let go and give ourselves a little space and freedom.

Today, even if just for a few minutes, find ways to release control and give yourself to frivolous play. Consider a fun family board game. Pick up a musical instrument to play or make a family band—that's what we do. Grab your tennis racket or make your way to a pool. Throw a Frisbee in your front yard. Take the time to play. See if it doesn't refresh you, restore your mind, and give you new energy to enter back into a busy world.

# ✎ Reflect ✎

WHEN WAS THE LAST TIME YOU ALLOWED YOURSELF TO PLAY,
TO BE FRIVOLOUS AND EVEN A BIT SILLY? HOW DID IT FEEL? HOW
MIGHT YOU INCORPORATE MORE OF THOSE MOMENTS INTO
YOUR LIFE?

# 33

# Taking a Risk

God is working in you, giving you the desire
and the power to do what pleases him.

PHILIPPIANS 2:13 NLT

For Gabe and me, the adoption conversation surfaced for about thirty minutes every three years after Kennedy was born. But we never quite felt the timing was right. We were maxed out, always on the move, and doing our best to live and work in a two-bedroom apartment.

When we moved to Tennessee, we considered adoption again, this time feeling a little more margin in our lives. Still, we weren't ready and kept kicking the conversation down the road.

Meanwhile, Kennedy imagined she'd have a baby sister, and she wasn't shy about asking for one. She didn't just ask, though.

She prayed and prayed for a baby sister. In fact, she had since she was five.

Kennedy's prayers over the years must have worked because one day I surrendered it all. "If this is something you want to happen," I prayed, "please bring her to me. Please put her right in front of my face, and I'll name her Joy."

Three years later, on December 3, 2018, my dear friend Meredith in Beijing, China, texted me a photo of an adorable five-year-old grinning ear to ear, a child with Down syndrome. Meredith wrote, "This girl's file is going to the US tomorrow."

I responded, "She's adorable. What's her name?"

"Chara," she replied.

I gasped. "You mean the Greek word for *joy*?"

When I got Meredith's text, I wanted to run. We were days from celebrating twenty years of marriage, and visions of growing independence danced in my head. I remember telling Gabe, full of fear, "This feels like the day I got Cade's diagnosis. The day everything changed for our future, and we started a life different than what we imagined."

Then it hit me. "Perhaps God gave us Cade because he knew seventeen years later he'd give us Joy, and we'd say yes." Gabe held me while I cried tears of surrender. This was indeed an invitation into something more. Instead of being empty nesters, we'd be heading back to kindergarten.

As I write this, it's the first week of December—exactly one year after Meredith sent that life-changing text—and we're at the end of the adoption

> Then it hit me. "Perhaps God gave us Cade because he knew seventeen years later he'd give us Joy, and we'd say yes."

process. We're in Guangxi, China, and tomorrow is "Gotcha Day," the day our daughter, Joy Lyons, will join our family forever. This risk ends in beauty, the culmination of partnering with God to create a new reality for our family. And though I should be nervous, anxious, maybe even a bit panicky, I'm not. Why? Because tomorrow we enter God's story for Joy, and we couldn't be more grateful.

Taking a risk may be the hardest thing you'll ever do, but it's the only way to partner with God in creating good and beautiful things. And as you partner with him in creating a life of faith, you'll learn to "not worry about tomorrow, for tomorrow will worry about itself."[1] You'll learn to live in the peace and joy of God's purpose for you.

## ✼ Reflect ✼

IS THERE A RISK YOU'VE BEEN AVOIDING, SOMETHING YOU KNOW GOD MIGHT BE CALLING YOU TO DO? WHAT IS KEEPING YOU FROM STEPPING INTO THAT CALLING? IS IT FEAR—OF REJECTION, OF FAILURE, OF THE UNKNOWN? SPEND SOME TIME IN REFLECTION AND JOURNALING. ASK GOD TO GIVE YOU THE COURAGE TO TAKE A RISK, TO PARTNER WITH HIM.

# 34

## Creating Beauty

"Build houses and settle down; plant
gardens and eat what they produce."

JEREMIAH 29:5

I t was on Gabe's to-do list for the new year to plant a garden.
For Christmas he requested books on all things gardening,
plant rotation, and how to harvest maple syrup. I'm not a country girl, so these hobbies aren't in my wheelhouse. I didn't grow
up getting my hands dirty, and other than helping water flowers
with a garden hose, I've never been praised for having a green
thumb.

Fast-forward three months and Gabe's Christmas wish
seemed prophetic. With a global pandemic coming our way and
a run on food wiping out grocery-store shelves, this notion of

a garden seemed somewhat reasonable. I was convinced, but what did I know about gardening? Besides sowing seeds, pulling weeds, and harvesting vegetables, not much. But I knew if we were going to do this, it needed to be beautiful.

I'm not sure what it is about my personality, but I've always loved design. Like all of us, I'm drawn to beautiful places. Some of them are natural—like a sunset or ocean waves—crafted by the hand of God. Then there are others, the type of beauty cultivated by human hands. Whether it's a work of art, a well-crafted home, or a landscape with flowers and trees, this blend of God's beauty intersecting with man's imagination is my sweet spot.

We are meant to cultivate beauty. This is core to how God's designed us. The fulfillment we receive from working with our hands, creating art, and cultivating natural resources into beautiful things is glorious. It makes me sad when I hear people say they aren't "creative." It's impossible because God created each of us in his image, and his creativity is unmatched.

> **We are meant to cultivate beauty.**

As children we were all creators, but life has a way of dampening our confidence. The subtle judgment of another or the refrain that creativity isn't practical can ring in our ears. But these lies hold us back from experiencing one of the most intimate ways God uses us in the world.

Together, Gabe and I designed our garden. We got out his sketch pad and started drawing. With measuring tapes criss-crossing our backyard, we began to envision the perfect layout to fit naturally between our home and garage. Taking inspiration from Gabe's friend Andrew, we set out to "build it like it will be here in one hundred years."

Then the work began. The first step was the installation of raised beds made of thick eastern red cedar. Then the archways and trellises were raised, creating space for cucumbers, tomatoes, and sugar peas to climb and suspend. The mushroom compost was stirred into organic soil and dumped into the beds before the fun of planting seeds began.

Perhaps the hardest, most rewarding part of the job was installing the flagstone pathway. Like a jigsaw puzzle, each piece would be carefully chosen, laid, and leveled to achieve precision. I even convinced Gabe to place the finishing touches of draping garden lights from roof to roof.

While it took three months from inception to completion, the effort to create a magical space we would enjoy was well worth it. The convenient design next to our home ensures easy access for simple weeding and harvest. The smooth stone path allows the kids to walk barefoot in the early mornings and discover their own taste for ripe cherry tomatoes right off the vine. While creating beauty takes time, effort, and imagination, the fruit of the reward is well worth it.

## ✺ Reflect ✺

WHAT ARE YOUR FAVORITE GOD-CREATED OR MAN-MADE EXPERIENCES OF BEAUTY? WHEN WAS THE LAST TIME YOU GOT YOUR HANDS DIRTY TO CREATE SOMETHING BEAUTIFUL? HOW DID THAT FEEL? MAYBE YOU'VE ALWAYS DREAMED OF MAKING POTTERY OR TRYING WOODWORKING, BUT YOU NEVER TOOK THE NEXT STEP. OR YOU WANT TO LEARN TO MAKE KOREAN FOOD. PERHAPS THERE'S AN OLD INSTRUMENT LYING DORMANT IN ITS CASE. TAKE ONE STEP THIS WEEK TOWARD COMMITTING TO CREATIVITY. SKETCH A PLAN FOR HOW YOU WANT TO INVEST IN YOUR CREATIVITY OVER THE NEXT SIX MONTHS. MAKE IT DOABLE, MAKE IT FUN.

# 35

# New Learning

Let the wise listen and add to their learning.

PROVERBS 1:5

Two months after arriving in New York City, we sent our youngest off to kindergarten. Just like that, our proverbial decade of weekdays at the library for story time, food court lunches, and children's museum playdates had drawn to a close.

I wasn't sad about this shift, though I felt the void. Looking back, I wonder if the anxiety I experienced that first year in Manhattan could be traced back to my not knowing what to do now that I had time. When we are uncertain about our place in the world, fear can settle in, and that's what happened to me. When faced with a clean slate, all I had were questions:

*Do I even deserve to spend time on myself?*

*What will I focus on in this new season?*
*How should I spend my newfound time?*
*Where do I start?*

It had been so long since I had time to consider what I enjoyed, what I wanted to do most. So I took inventory. Over the last decade, while not dealing with diapers, I loved reading up on the latest in fashion and interior design. It provided an escape into adult land and now was a clue into an area of untapped potential.

**When we are uncertain about our place in the world, fear can settle in, and that's what happened to me.**

Manhattan has some of the leading design schools in the country, so I signed up for The Fundamentals of Fashion Design. Every Friday evening, Gabe would care for the kids, and I'd jump on a train to Union Square to join the other creatives, designers, and artistic types, who were a lot like me but about half my age.

The Fundamentals of Fashion Design entailed fashion design history, drawing fashion flats, sketching live models, and doing a little costume design. I learned I was awful at sketching, but redemption came toward the end of the semester when we finally moved to pattern-making and sewing. I found my groove and made a soft, gray woolen dress with fitted bodice and pleated skirt. When I modeled it for the class of mostly twenty-year-olds, they gave me affirming applause—impressed that this old girl just might have a little *Vogue* in her after all.

Taking a class is a more formal way of learning something new, but one of my favorite ways is something author Julia Cameron calls "The Artist Date." She wrote,

> The Artist Date is a once-weekly, festive, solo expedition to explore something that interests you. The Artist Date need not be overtly "artistic"—think mischief more than mastery. Artist Dates fire up the imagination. They spark whimsy. They encourage play. Since art is about the play of ideas, they feed our creative work by replenishing our inner well of images and inspiration.[1]

When we give ourselves new experiences, we expand our thinking and creativity.

If you are in a dreary season and barely putting one foot in front of the other, you're not alone. I know how it feels. The last thing you want to hear is that you need to take on one more thing. But trust me, if you take the courageous step to learn something new, you'll find new pathways to freedom, pathways that lead you to become who you were meant to be.

# ❦ Reflect ❦

DOES THE IDEA OF THE ARTIST DATE APPEAL TO YOU? WHY?
WHAT SORTS OF EXPERIENCES WOULD YOU EXPLORE? MAKE A
DATE WITH YOURSELF THIS WEEK AND EXPLORE SOMETHING
NEW. THEN SPEND SOME TIME REFLECTING ON THE IMPACT IT
HAS ON YOU.

# 36

# Holy Inventory

Let us search out and examine our
ways, and turn back to the Lord.

LAMENTATIONS 3:40 NKJV

A few years back, my heart was arrested by Parker Palmer's book *Let Your Life Speak*.[1] It was the first book that challenged me to take inventory of my days and to consider my thoughts, actions, and daily routine. I began to ask myself, *Is the life I lead the life that longs to live in me?*

When I first asked myself this question, it seemed my life was swallowed by Pull-Ups and pacifiers and poop. Though these motherhood moments weren't the whole of my life's longing, they were largely the makeup of my days. I'd never stopped to consider the life that longed to live in me.

Fast-forward eighteen years, and we've moved from Pull-Ups to sports jerseys and athletic gear for summer camp. Raising teenagers comes with a boatload of bustle. But no matter the season, pausing to take inventory has saved my life. When I find myself too busy for it, I'm lost. When I make time for it, I gain critical perspective.

> **No matter the season, pausing to take inventory has saved my life.**

So what does taking inventory look like? I first start small. Every day I ask myself questions such as, *Where is God leading me? What new people has he placed in my path? What new commitment is he asking me to make?* I try to act on the obvious and immediate and to note any big revelations I may need to come back to when I have extended time.

I also set aside a few hours quarterly and take a deeper dive. I start by acknowledging all the pushes and pulls on my life. Using a rubric that helps keep it simple, I ask four simple questions I learned from Pete Richardson, mentor to Gabe and me:

- *What's right?* This question keeps me aware of and grateful for the gifts in my life.
- *What's wrong?* This allows me to assess and name the challenges I'm facing, taking time to name those things that

feel off or out of order. In naming what's wrong, I take the first step in solving my problems.

- *What's confused?* This helps me isolate the rabbit trails I seem to chase to no end. *Am I teaching our children respect and responsibility? Am I making friendships a priority? Is our time together as a family quality time?* When I carve out time to process my answers and write them down, the anxiety associated with these questions dissipates.
- *What's missing?* This requires a hard look at areas of life I may be too close to, areas I can't evaluate alone. I need insight from Gabe and a few trusted friends to help me identify blind spots or talk through my desires to ensure they are rooted in the story God has called me to live.

If we do our inventories right, it will be a holy process. When we rest long enough to take inventory, when we ask God to cultivate our hearts, talents, and passions according to the purpose he planned before our days began,[2] we'll find new horizons opening up, horizons beyond all we could ask or imagine.[3]

## ⤳ Reflect ⤲

SOCRATES SAID, "THE UNEXAMINED LIFE IS NOT WORTH LIVING." TAKE A FEW MOMENTS EACH DAY TO EXAMINE YOUR LIFE. WHAT ARE THE QUESTIONS THAT WOULD MAKE UP YOUR OWN DAILY INVENTORY? SET ASIDE TIME FOR DEEPER REFLECTION AS WELL, JOURNALING YOUR ANSWERS TO *WHAT'S RIGHT?*, *WHAT'S WRONG?*, *WHAT'S CONFUSED?*, AND *WHAT'S MISSING?*

# 37

# Turn Off the Tech

Am I now seeking the approval of man,
or of God? Or am I trying to please
man? If I were still trying to please man,
I would not be a servant of Christ.

GALATIANS 1:10 ESV

I started using Instagram on May 7, 2011, to be exact. Though many of my friends were active on social networking platforms, I was not a savvy social-media user. But the idea of keeping a real-time photo journal to share with friends and family? This was something I could get behind. After one weekend, I was hooked.

But what began as memory making became a compulsion to share. Gabe noticed before I did. "You don't need to capture *everything*; just enjoy the moment!" he said. Kennedy, my daughter, saw it too and would ask, "Can you stop looking at your phone?"

In the spring of 2018, I felt God whispering that I should fast from social media. I dismissed and defended my actions. *It's no big deal, God. It doesn't mean that much to me.* But I woke up a few weeks later feeling an urge, a conviction even, to press pause for a season. I couldn't wait another day.

> **In the spring of 2018, I felt God whispering that I should fast from social media.**

When I jumped off social media, things changed. First, I started dreaming again. On the back porch, journal in hand, new ideas and thoughts flooded my mind. Second, I was sleeping better than ever, my mind and body catching up on much-needed rest. And third, my passion for learning returned as I read more books, listened to more podcasts and talks.

A month into this fast, I drove around a bend in the road and gasped at the sky, ablaze with pinks and reds. Normally, I would have pulled over and angled for the perfect shot. That's when God reminded me of this truth: "You are worthy to receive something beautiful, and you don't have to share it."

What began as a break from the constant churn of social media became a fundamental lesson in worthiness. I came to see that my worth is not found in approval "out there." It is found in the loving gifts God offers in the "right now," in the intimate invitation of a sunset.

When I did reenter social media, it was with caution. I didn't want to lose the slower pace of life I'd found or my longer attention span and diminishing need for public approval. I can see the flicker in my Kennedy's eyes as she shares something from her day, and I give her my whole attention. I catch our son Cade's goofy smirk when he's up to no good. By resting from social media, I've recovered the lost art of *paying attention*, and somehow, that has brought me a sense of peace and tranquility.

Consider taking your own social media fast. Leave your smartphone in a box by the front door when you walk in after a long day. Limit the number of texts you send in a day. Give your mind, soul, and body the rest they need—for your sake and for the sake of those around you.

# ✈ Reflect ✈

FOR THE NEXT FEW DAYS, KEEP A LOG OF YOUR TIME ON SOCIAL MEDIA. DOES THE AMOUNT OF TIME SURPRISE YOU? WHAT OTHER THINGS MIGHT FILL YOUR TIME INSTEAD—THINGS YOU DON'T BELIEVE YOU HAVE "TIME" FOR? CHALLENGE YOURSELF TO TAKE A BREAK FROM SOCIAL MEDIA. WHAT CHANGES DO YOU HOPE THAT WILL BRING TO YOUR LIFE?

# 38

# Your Calling

As a prisoner for the Lord, then,
I urge you to live a life worthy of
the calling you have received.

EPHESIANS 4:1

A dear friend and mentor, Pete, once said to me, "Calling isn't limited to vocation, it's rooted in God's creativity and how he's designed us."

As I considered the truth of his words, I realized our purpose began when God formed us, and he continues to call us as long as we have breath. The psalmist wrote it this way: "For you created my inmost being; you knit me together in my mother's womb. I praise you because I am fearfully and wonderfully made; your works are wonderful, I know that full well."[1] God appointed his purpose for each of us, even in our mothers' wombs. God isn't casual about establishing our talents; he ordained them before our days began.[2]

I considered the uniqueness of my own story, the path I'd taken from the womb, and as I did, I began to understand my calling. Before I was born, God knew I'd be a reader; he knew that in fourth grade I'd read sixty-two Nancy Drew books. He knew I'd be mesmerized by the power of a good story. He knew the reader in me would long to communicate, to tell stories. God knew I'd major in mass communications in college, that I'd love the art of sharing messages.

God knew more than my passions and talents, though. He also knew the ways mental illness would unfurl in my family. He knew I'd give birth to a child with special needs. He knew I'd suffer from panic disorder. But the story didn't end with my limitations and weaknesses. God also knew he'd equip me to use my gifts to share hope with others through my own brokenness.

As I unpacked my story and my unique gifts, I began to understand. *Calling is where our talents and burdens collide.* As I shared this clarity with Gabe, it became obvious to both of us. I should start writing. God wanted me to share his words with a hurting, needy world. God—the very God who formed me, who breathed life into me, who knew what I was capable of handling—would empower me for the work.

As children of God, we have a corporate calling to love God and make him known. What's amazing is that this calling looks different for each of us based on our talents and

> As I unpacked my story and my unique gifts, I began to understand. *Calling is where our talents and burdens collide.*

the burdens we feel for others. We don't have to stress about finding our "thing" but simply ask God to reveal his plans for us.

Callings are not one size fits all. Some of you may be called to teach, speak, and write. Others may be called to serve in the corporate world, or at home, or with your church youth group. You may be called to serve in quiet ways or in ways that go unrecognized.

No matter your calling, God chose you and appointed a purpose for you well before you were born. This purpose is to bring glory to Jesus, to be his very hands and feet. And if the task is daunting, remember this: as he calls you, he leans in and whispers, "Don't worry; I'll empower your work."

# Reflect

"CALLING IS WHERE OUR TALENTS AND BURDENS COLLIDE." WHAT GIFTS AND TALENTS HAS GOD GIVEN YOU? WHAT BURDENS BREAK YOUR HEART? IN JOURNALING AND PRAYER, ASK GOD TO GUIDE YOU TO THE PLACE WHERE THEY COLLIDE AND TO LEAD YOU INTO LIVING OUT HIS CALLING ON YOUR LIFE.

Say

to Others

# 39

# Set Free

It is for freedom that Christ has set us free.
Stand firm, then, and do not let yourselves
be burdened again by a yoke of slavery.

GALATIANS 5:1

All my life I've run the hamster wheel of achievement and acceptance; a headstrong, type-A control freak, looking for love. As a child I earned love by working hard to fit in. At church I earned love by memorizing verses. At school I earned love by pleasing teachers. Looking back, I see a girl in pigtails, acceptance her endgame.

In kindergarten, I repeated the sinner's prayer before I could write complete sentences. I memorized King James verses with words like *sanctification, edification,* and *fornication.* I regurgitated the definition of *justification*—"Just-as-if-I-hadn't-sinned"—even though I didn't understand what the words meant. I absorbed all this burdensome religion like a six-, seven-, and eight-year-old sponge, and furthermore, I believed it must be true, all of it.

A chameleon of sorts, I learned the ways of fitting in, of popularity, and of being liked, all the while grasping for permission to be fully known and, in spite of that, fully loved. But what about freedom? The God I was striving for was rigid and lifeless and seemed far away. And although I believed he was real, I wasn't convinced he was good. So I went on trying to be the best version of myself, hoping maybe I'd catch a glimpse of his approval.

Whenever I felt rejected or insecure, I buckled down with strategies to be more confident, more accepted, and more loved. I watched what others were doing and adopted their games. But the more I learned, the more fraudulent it all appeared. I read freedom in the pages of Scripture, but it felt elusive and temporary. I wore myself ragged trying to be enough, and it wore me out. I longed to be free.

Then, many months ago, I walked a Florida beach at sunset, watching the last sliver of crimson sun slip under the waves, far out on the horizon. Streaky pinks and golds

> I wore myself ragged trying to be enough, and it wore me out. I longed to be free.

burned into my mind, unlocking my memory of rhythm. And there, on the beach, I danced.

And there, in the twisting and twirling, I felt a glimpse of the freedom God longed for me to live into, a reckless abandon blooming into unencumbered joy. As the wind picked up under the cotton-candy sky, I pictured the Almighty looking down, eyes landing on his little girl leaping on the beach. Spontaneous and awkward, though I didn't care, I embraced this moment alone with him at dusk. *This is what freedom feels like. This is the way I was meant to live,* I thought. *This is the miracle of grace.*

When we become enslaved to anything—achievement, approval, popularity, even religion—we miss out on a life of surrender and peace. A life where we experience the truth that God is enough. A life where God is the Good Shepherd who gives us everything we need. A life where we lack nothing.

Jesus wants to relieve you of this world's weight. He's waiting, just beyond the horizon, for you to be ready. He will come.

He will teach you to be free. Say yes to his freedom.

# ✤ Reflect ✤

WHAT IS ENSLAVING YOU AND KEEPING YOU FROM EXPERIENCING ALL THE FREEDOM CHRIST HAS TO OFFER? ARE YOU READY TO THROW IT OFF, STEP INTO THE LIGHT, AND DANCE IN THE FREEDOM OF CHRIST? ASK GOD TO HELP YOU STEP INTO THE FREEDOM HE WANTS YOU TO LIVE IN.

# 40

# The Way of Forgiveness

"In your anger do not sin": Do not let the
sun go down while you are still angry,
and do not give the devil a foothold.

EPHESIANS 4:26–27

Gabe and I both have intense personalities. As a firstborn trailblazer, I made my way, worked forty hours a week to pay for college, and later funded our wedding while most of my friends were enjoying college fun. Side note, I did sneak in fun, just a little less sleep!

Gabe is entrepreneurial, a savvy and smart risk-taker, strong in confidence and sharing his opinion. In fact, we found fifteen years into marriage, we both have an opinion on virtually everything. From landscaping decisions to living room configurations—there are few moments we defer to the other. Is it exhausting? Sometimes. Is it boring? Never. This produced an iron-sharpening-iron relationship, with ramifications we didn't see coming until it was almost too late.

Every marriage experiences friction, but wounds in our most trusted relationships plant seeds of resentment, which lead to death. Most marriages don't end because of a dramatic fight but from a steady growth of unforgiveness, bitterness, and contempt. Contempt is a killer. The belief you are better than your spouse and they are lucky to have you? These thoughts bring death to any relationship.

Jesus invites us to cast our burdens and resentments on him. We weren't meant to carry the wounds that have deeply hurt us in our relationships. We all have the propensity to sin, to miss the mark, to say hurtful words or tear others down. Many times these statements stir out of our own insecurities and unhealed wounds. We cannot give what we have not received.

Have you had one of those nights where you went to bed angry? I have. You toss and turn, restless and unresolved at three a.m. until the early morning hours, where the hurt feels more palpable. Dawn appears with

> We weren't meant to carry the wounds that have deeply hurt us in our relationships.

less patience and grace than you felt the evening before, and thus the cycle of misunderstanding grows.

Paul offered practical advice to each of us about the importance of living in forgiveness. Surrendering to forgiveness daily is a practice, a rhythm we must embrace. Not just for the person who has wronged us but for our own mental health. It's not good for our souls to go to bed angry.[1]

During a marriage intensive twenty years in, Gabe and I began to see the resentments we had held on to for years. Buried deep below the busyness of daily life and accommodation, we discovered past hurts that kept us from deep levels of intimacy. As God revealed these truths, we got on our knees and confessed. We repented and asked each other for forgiveness and, in tears, embraced. We knew in our own strength we could never move into freedom without the forgiveness of Christ washing over us.

We went to bed that night in full embrace, the sun having set on our past resentments, ready to rise for our new beginning.

# ✵ Reflect ✵

WHAT PAST HURTS HAVE TURNED INTO RESENTMENTS IN YOUR PRESENT RELATIONSHIPS? ASK CHRIST TO SHOW YOU THE AREAS WHERE YOU'VE HELD ON TO GRIEVANCES THAT NEED TO BE FORGIVEN. CREATE SPACE EACH WEEKEND WHEN YOU GET AN HOUR ALONE TO SHARE WITH YOUR SPOUSE, OUT OF A HEART OF CONFESSION, ANY GRIEVANCES YOU'VE HELD ON TO AND WANT TO RELEASE. INVITE GOD TO DO A HEALING WORK, TO BRING FULL FORGIVENESS AND CHART A NEW WAY FORWARD.

# 41

# The Gift of Hugs

*The touch of his hand healed every one.*

LUKE 4:40 NLT

My son Cade sees the world through a rose-tinted Down syndrome lens. He's never met a stranger, and if someone seems a little out of sorts, his remedy is a good old-fashioned hug.

One particular spring morning in New York, we'd timed our train ride poorly. Rush hour in Manhattan's subways is from another world. With people crammed in wall-to-wall like sardines, finding a place to hold on was going to be a turf battle. Cade hates standing up in trains. His balance isn't the best, and the way the express trains sway and bounce, he all but demands a seat.

Holding to the center pole, he quietly scanned the seats for any sign of a gap. It didn't need to be much, any sliver of blue fiberglass bench peeking from between two riders and he'd take his shot. He found it, then darted for a crevice that couldn't have been more than six inches wide. After turning his bottom around, he wedged himself between the hips of two female riders. The younger brunette to his left, music blasting through her headphones, shot an annoyed glance at Cade. The other, an older lady trying to read a book, recognized Cade's innocent look and obliged.

Cade's pretty aware that his not-so-sly moves can create annoyances. So after securing his seat, he grinned and tapped the shoulder of the brunette next to him. He offered an exaggerated wave, as if saying, "I'm here now, let's be friends." She recognized Cade wasn't your average fare rider and allowed herself a kind grin. Sensing a hint of approval, he then made his move, put his arm around her for a side hug, tilted his head, and gave her his biggest smile. She took out her earbuds and started up a cute chitchat.

The older lady realized she was missing out on all the fun and leaned in for her own side hug, Cade happy to oblige. Cade's courage to break the typical rules of maintaining personal space yet again made him a couple of new friends and brightened their day.

Physical touch picks me up, but it's not just me. All of us

need physical touch. God created us for love and comfort, and he wants us to communicate that love and comfort to others. Of course, not everyone is a hugger, but in reaching for the hand of a friend or offering the reassuring squeeze of an arm, we remind one another we don't have to do life alone.

> God created us for love and comfort, and he wants us to communicate that love and comfort to others.

Jesus displayed the power of healing touch over and over, but he also used touch as a way of blessing and receiving blessing. From blessing the children to his forgiveness of the woman whose tears washed his feet, Jesus used physical touch as a gateway to healing, blessing, and connection with others and with God.[1]

Are you needing the tender encouragement of a gentle touch today? Find a loved one—your spouse, a family member, a friend—and ask for a hug. See if it doesn't mute the anxiety, the depression, the pain. And if you know someone who is struggling, offer them a hug (a good, long one). Let them know they are not alone. See if that kind of physical touch doesn't bring relief.

## ⋙ Reflect ⋘

THINK ABOUT THE LAST *REAL* HUG YOU RECEIVED. HOW DID IT LEAVE YOU FEELING? WHO ARE THE PEOPLE YOU CAN TURN TO FOR HUGS AND SUPPORTIVE, ENCOURAGING TOUCHES? WHO, IN TURN, CAN YOU GIFT WITH THE COMFORT AND ENCOURAGEMENT OF YOUR TOUCH?

# 42

# I'm Sorry

Confess your sins to each other and pray
for each other so that you may be healed.

JAMES 5:16

Just before exams one autumn, I had grand Thursday night
plans. It was our family's only weeknight together between
play practice, youth group, and swim team, and I'd made a
home-cooked meal. I tried to spark conversation, but no one
had anything to offer but worn looks and fatigued attitudes.
Within minutes, the evening disintegrated into finger-pointing
and complaining.

Unsure how to salvage the night, Gabe and I reacted the way
we always do when we're unsure what else to do: "Go to your
room!" But as our kids mumbled responses and began walking

upstairs, hearts more distant with each step, I knew banishing them to their rooms wasn't the right move. The best response when connection is broken is not to push away but rather the opposite, to pull in.

I yelled up to them, "Stop! Come back to the living room." With eye rolls and complaints about my inconsistent parenting, they returned. Undeterred, I launched into conversation.

> The best response when connection is broken is not to push away but rather the opposite, to pull in.

"None of us feel like being together right now or want to have a conversation about how to address the tension and conflict." The kids didn't say anything, and I imagined them thinking to themselves, *Exactly, so why are we here?*

I continued, "What if we try something else? Let's worship together, singing something before God and one another that is good and true. I know singing is the last thing you want to do right now, but if we want to reunite our hearts, this might be the best way to work through something instead of faking it and moving on."

Those initial moments were awkward for sure, but no one had a better idea. Pierce, always happy to do the helpful thing, grabbed his guitar and began playing. Within a few minutes, everyone relaxed and settled into the song. We fixed our focus outside of ourselves and reoriented our hearts.

When the second song came to a close, Gabe and I couldn't get the words out fast enough. We both apologized for letting the conversation get out of hand. By the end of the third song, our kids opened up about the baggage they'd brought with them into the night and apologized for their own part in the drama. Hugs and laughter returned, and we felt more connected than we had in weeks.

Scripture says, "Do not let the sun go down while you are still angry, and do not give the devil a foothold."[1]

An intruder doesn't need our whole heart, just a foothold—a crack wide enough to get a foot in the door. When we hold grudges, keeping a record of wrongs, that crack becomes a wide-open door for the enemy to do what he does best: "steal and kill and destroy" the ones we love most.[2] Apologizing paves the way for forgiveness in our relationships and sucks anger, anxiety, and stress out of the room.

If you know you've played a part in a broken relationship, why not lead with a heartfelt apology? Ask for forgiveness. Then rest easy, knowing you've laid the first stone on the path to restored connections.

# Reflect

DO YOU STRUGGLE TO APOLOGIZE, EVEN WHEN YOU KNOW YOU ARE IN THE WRONG? WHAT HOLDS YOU BACK? ARE THERE RELATIONSHIPS IN YOUR LIFE THAT COULD USE AN APOLOGY? ASK GOD TO GIVE YOU THE HEART AND COURAGE TO SAY, "I'M SORRY."

# 43

# Open Porches and Open Doors

"Truly I tell you, whatever you did for
one of the least of these brothers and
sisters of mine, you did for me."

MATTHEW 25:40

Come on over, and bring the whole family; we can't wait to see you!" These are words I never tire of hearing. The welcome of friends who feel like family welcoming me in, no matter the season, time of night, or need—it offers a relief that is rare in our world.

My cousins, the Scarberry family, are lifelong teachers of this kind of open-door hospitality. Going all the way back to my childhood, every memory I have of visiting their family is full of warmth and welcome. My uncle Rick and aunt Martha lived with an infectious spirit of generosity that they passed down to the next generation. Today their fortysomething-year-old children carry on their legacy.

Families like the Scarberrys are the epitome of fun. They believe *more* is better, and *now* is just as good as tomorrow. They share their abundance and remind me how the true power of connection takes place when we welcome others into our lives and spaces. I don't know about you, but this is the kind of family I want to have.

Gabe and I continue to be inspired by this open-door policy, so when we saw our home in Franklin for the first time, we knew it'd be a perfect fit for our family. It had a long, wide front porch, and we could envision it as a place for family and friends to gather.

From the first blooms of spring to the final leaves of autumn, we get full use out of this porch. We've hosted board meetings and impromptu birthday parties, watched firefly catching on summer evenings at dusk, and shared lemonade with friends traveling through town. Just the other day, our friend Tim set up a painting station, a tin of watercolors in hand. I've prayed with friends on our rocking chairs as they were preparing to move to a new city, cried tears as my mother-in-law shared her journey of becoming cancer-free, and reflected on fond moments with my sister as we processed the death of our dad. When the cold creeps in, we move the fellowship indoors. Whether it's afternoon cookie decorating with teen girls, an impromptu coffee or brunch, or a festive "friendsgiving potluck," everyone huddles around the kitchen island, eager to connect.

Hospitality doesn't require an elaborate meal or making sure every nook and cranny is clean. People crave connection, even if the house isn't perfectly put together. Creating a sustainable culture of hospitality requires casual frequency, getting together often, coming as you are, hosting as you are.

> **Hospitality doesn't require an elaborate meal or making sure every nook and cranny is clean.**

Jon Tyson, our pastor from New York, says, "Biblical hospitality is an environment of welcome where a person's identity goes from an outsider to an insider so they can belong. It's turning the other into 'one another.'" Isn't that what we all crave? Shifting from being *the other* to becoming *one another*? I want to make it my mission to help people belong.

When I open my home, extending hospitality, I live into the generosity of God's design. Pressure and stress melt away. Through hospitality, I find true community, connection with friends, family, and those we now love or soon will because I made myself available and opened our doors.

# Reflect

DO YOU FEEL COMFORTABLE OPENING YOUR HOME IN HOSPITALITY? IF NOT, WHY NOT? CHALLENGE YOURSELF TO HOST A GATHERING—IMPROMPTU AND IMPERFECT—AND NOTE HOW IT MAKES YOU AND YOUR GUESTS FEEL.

# 44

# Welcoming Vulnerability

"My grace is sufficient for you, for my
power is made perfect in weakness."

2 CORINTHIANS 12:9

A few months back I met some friends for impromptu burgers
and fries, and in my attempt to let off some steam, I shared
a bit more intimately than was appropriate for this particular
group setting. I immediately wanted to take back my last couple
of sentences, but there they were, hanging out there, for everyone
to take in. My attempt to confide went sideways. I couldn't get to
my car fast enough.

I learned that day to be thoughtful about *what* to share, *when*
to share, and *with whom* to share. Group settings aren't always
the best places for vulnerable conversations that require more

explanation. You can risk being misunderstood at best, judged at worst.

As you develop your own trusted circle, as you find the right people, keep revealing your deepest self with them. After all, while vulnerability with the wrong sorts of folks fosters feelings of inferiority and judgment, vulnerability with the right people brings trust, bolsters our feelings of love, and brings hope.

I have a handful of girlfriends who have taught me the power of vulnerability. Some I've known since high school, while others I met in my twenties. These friends have helped me when I needed comfort and challenged me when I needed confrontation. When I opened up about my anxiety and panic years ago, they met me in my most vulnerable place and helped me believe wholeness was possible. And though the text thread topics have moved on from toddler life to our newbie teen drivers having fender benders, we are committed to showing up.

> Vulnerability with the right people brings trust, bolsters our feelings of love, and brings hope.

The thing that has kept me close to each of these women is their willingness to be vulnerable. There's a safety in walking through highs and lows over the years, in giving and receiving grace. In so many ways, their friendships have reflected to me what God's love looks and feels like over the long haul. God invites me to share vulnerably with him, to lay it all bare, and as I do, he becomes my safe place, my refuge. He frees me from the opinions of others and the worries of my own heart. He shows me how to receive abundantly so I can serve others, not out of my strength but his. He teaches me how to make space for the vulnerability of others too.

Perhaps you've tried to share your heart with a trusted friend, parent, or spouse, and somewhere along the way you were shamed for those feelings. Instead of being held, cherished, and understood, you felt the sting of betrayal. I know this pain, but that doesn't mean we should stop being vulnerable. The enemy of our souls wants us to be isolated and alone because these feelings make us easy prey. Why? When we're alone and vulnerable, we feel afraid. When we're together and vulnerable, we become brave.

Make the effort to connect—really connect in true vulnerability—with those you love. Your courage to bring your whole, beautiful self out into the open just might inspire them to do the same. In that vulnerable connection, you'll bolster each other's courage, give each other love, and point each other to God, who can strengthen you even in the darkest hour.

# Reflect

HAVE YOU ALLOWED YOURSELF TO BE VULNERABLE WITH THOSE YOU LOVE, WITH THOSE WHO LOVE YOU? OR DO YOU TEND TO HOLD BACK YOUR WHOLE, AUTHENTIC SELF? FIND ONE PERSON YOU TRUST, REACH OUT TO THEM THIS WEEK, AND SAY WHAT'S ON YOUR HEART. ASK THEM WHAT'S ON THEIRS. PRAY THAT GOD WOULD ALLOW SECURITY IN YOUR RELATIONSHIPS SO THAT THIS CONFESSIONAL PRACTICE BECOMES MORE REGULAR AND JOYFUL.

# 45

# Extravagant Love

Trust steadily in God, hope
unswervingly, love extravagantly.
And the best of the three is love.

1 CORINTHIANS 13:13 THE MESSAGE

Gabe and I had just celebrated eighteen years of marriage, and in line with our conviction that we needed to reestablish ourselves and our relationship, we committed to engage in a few couples counseling sessions.

To be fair, I thought we were doing pretty well. But ninety minutes into the session, it was clear there would be no pats on the back. Instead, the counselor urged us to dig deeper into our history and explore some areas we'd managed to cover up. So we did.

Looking back, I discovered that while I was growing up, I'd felt unknown in some key relationships. As a result, I always withheld a small percentage of my heart. If things didn't work out, I was determined I wouldn't be the one left hurting.

So, when Gabe and I were dating and he told me he was falling in love with me, my heart leapt and then nosedived within seconds. I wanted to hear his declaration of love but was also deathly afraid of the risk involved. And I finally blurted out, "I don't know how to love."

My words hung in the air. Gabe held me close as tears streamed down my cheeks and said without batting an eyelash, "I'm going to teach you how to love."

Twenty years later, we remembered how that conversation marked a significant shift in our relationship. I didn't harbor a single doubt for the rest of our dating days about Gabe, about us, or about marriage. I knew his fateful words did not come from his own strength or zeal, but with an assurance that can only come from Christ.

> Gabe held me close as tears streamed down my cheeks and said without batting an eyelash, "I'm going to teach you how to love."

But that day, during our session, I realized I still wasn't completely free to love. Fragments of rejection from the first half of my life still held me captive. And when things got stressful or hard, those wounds were exposed.

The counselor asked me to explain in more detail, and I proceeded with caution. I explained how when Gabe challenges me, I immediately become defensive. I perceive anything other than praise as criticism or rejection.

The counselor looked me in the eye and gently, but firmly, said, "Rebekah, the goal is to hear something challenging and not break relationship. Running and hiding is an unhealthy response. Staying intimately connected—even when the feedback is not what you want to hear—will be critical to your and Gabe's relationship growth."

After our counseling session that evening, I reread 1 Corinthians 13, knelt on my carpet, and asked Jesus again to heal my heart and help me to love.

I wanted *more* of Christ's love for my husband, our children, and my friends. I wanted freedom from the bondage of anger, unforgiveness, and bitterness—strongholds that were keeping me from loving as Christ loves.

It wasn't just Gabe and my family I wanted to love more. I wanted to love the overlooked, the outcast, and the discarded. I considered all these people and prayed, "Lead me into the freedom to love as you love."

As my prayers spilled out, Christ's kindness overtook me

and love spilled from his heart into mine. The more I received his love, the more I wanted to love others. And isn't that how everything with Jesus works? He is gracious to give when we ask.

# ❧ Reflect ❧

DO YOU FEEL FREE TO LOVE FEROCIOUSLY, COMPLETELY, AND WITHOUT RESERVATION? OR IS SOMETHING HOLDING YOU BACK? DIVE INTO SCRIPTURE AND READ ABOUT GOD'S LOVE FOR YOU. RECORD THE TRUTHS YOU FIND THERE, AND ASK GOD TO USE THEM TO SET YOU FREE TO LOVE AS HE LOVES.

# 46

## True Connection

Not giving up meeting together,
as some are in the habit of doing,
but encouraging one another.

HEBREWS 10:25

I t was a scary time to get on an airplane. Our premature new-born was only five weeks into the world, and traveling was not recommended. With his low birth weight, Down syndrome diagnosis, and sluggish appetite, leaving the safety of home felt risky. But a family wedding had been on the calendar for a year. And more than anything, my heart needed the connection. Reeling from the most difficult weeks of our young married life, we knew we needed to take a proactive but risky step. After all, the human soul needs connection more than anything else.

> **The human soul needs connection more than anything else.**

Three years into marriage, the enthusiasm to bring new life into the world was dampened.

My final ultrasound revealed our baby was in danger, and I was given one directive—rush to the hospital. After the traumatic process of being quickly admitted, preparation for an emergency C-section began. With no time to waste and the baby's heart rate dropping to sixty beats per minute, the epidural had barely kicked in when surgery commenced. Minutes later, Cade Christian Lyons was born at 4.9 pounds and immediately put into the neonatal intensive care unit. He would live there for one week until he gained the strength to carry on at home.

After many weeks of living in survival mode, I was exhausted. Everything in me wanted to camp out at home. Staying in my robe and slippers, eating meals delivered by the best of friends, was comforting. But my soul was starved for adult conversation. What I needed most was to see our extended family at my future brother-in-law's wedding.

Risking to connect is crucial, especially when loneliness is at an all-time high. Zoom connects and FaceTime calls help us keep up with those we love, but there is no replacement for being in the same room. As Stanford Medicine researcher Dr. Emma Seppala reported, "People who feel more connected to others have lower levels of anxiety and depression. Moreover, studies show they also have higher self-esteem, greater empathy for others, are more trusting and cooperative and, as a consequence, others are more open to trusting and cooperating with them. In other words, social connectedness generates a positive feedback loop of social, emotional and physical well-being."[1]

The idea of embodiment is biblical. It goes back to the story of the Father sending his Son, Jesus, to take on human flesh. Jesus would not be just a spirit, or an idea, but his life would become the model for how we are to live in the world. He lived in community with disciples; traveling together, sharing meals, surviving threats, and pursuing a common purpose bonded them. He would be Emmanuel, God *with* us.

The writer of Hebrews saw connection so vital that, even while under the threat of death, he implored the church to gather.[2] He wanted them to be in the same room, embodied, encouraging one another, which quite literally means to "put courage in." Something happens when we gather in the same space, even if it means taking a risk.

As we arrived at the wedding destination, we jumped out of our car to greet our family and friends with sheer joy. Cade was the first grandson for Gabe's parents, and the excitement that he would be part of the festivities, even if in a car seat, was enough to make new grandparents beam. Our weekend was magical, and as we enjoyed the reception with little Cade sound asleep as the music rocked, we were glad we decided true connection was worth the risk.

# ❧ Reflect ❧

HAS FEAR STOPPED YOU FROM PURSUING CONNECTION?
WHAT ARE CREATIVE WAYS YOU CAN PRIORITIZE PERSONAL
CONNECTION? OUR SOULS WERE MEANT FOR CONNECTION,
AND IT PRODUCES POSITIVE EFFECTS ON OUR EMOTIONAL,
PHYSICAL, AND MENTAL HEALTH. NEXT TIME YOU FEEL ANXIOUS
OR LONELY, COMMIT TO REACH OUT TO A FRIEND AND LET THEM
KNOW YOU NEED CONNECTION.

# 47

# A Quiet Stillness

Jesus often withdrew to the
wilderness for prayer.

LUKE 5:16 NLT

Growing up, I always considered myself an extrovert. I never declined an invitation or opportunity to hang with friends. I was enthusiastic about life, and *the more the merrier* was my modus operandi. But when I became a mom of toddlers, I craved alone time. Closing the door to the bathroom felt sacred. When those toddlers became teens, I'd linger in the car for a few moments after they went inside. Instead of exercising in a noisy, crowded gym, I began to prefer morning workouts involving yoga and nature hikes. I spent large swaths of time at home, sitting in the quiet.

What did that mean? Was I becoming an introvert?

Discovering just how much I loved less noisy spaces, I picked up Susan Cain's book *Quiet,* in which she wrote, "Introverts . . . may have strong social skills and enjoy parties and business meetings, but after a while wish they were home in their pajamas. They prefer to devote their social energies to close friends, colleagues, and family."[1] She was describing at least a part of me to a T.

No matter what we call ourselves, all of us need quiet—times when we pause, reflect, and assess. In fact, Jesus often retreated into the mountains for solitude and prayer. Quiet was a part of his consistent routine—so how much more must *we* need it in our own lives?

But if you think getting quiet is easy, think again. The noise and distractions are endless in this digital age. Even if you clear out the distractions and create space for quiet, you'll have to get comfortable with yourself. But in the quiet we gain perspective. It helps us maintain a sense of calm, re-center, and become more fully who we were designed to be.

> No matter what we call ourselves, all of us need quiet—times when we pause, reflect, and assess.

As I incorporated intentional practices of quiet into my life, I noticed I was better able to connect with the people in my life and become a better friend.

How?

The quiet taught me to *listen* again. As I did, I asked genuine questions of my friends, and I stopped to connect with their hearts. Quiet listening also taught me to *discern*, to hear what was *not* being said. Finally, quiet listening taught me to *understand*. It taught me how to keep from filling every empty space with words and how to sit in quiet empathy for my spouse, friends, and children.[2]

When we carve out space for the quiet, to retreat to a silent place to pray, journal, or read, we rest from the noisy distractions of our lives. This rest pulls us out of the anxiety and stress of the world, if only for a moment. When we create spaces of quiet with others, it allows us to take a break from offering solutions or unwanted advice and allows us to show empathy, love, and understanding.

Quiet provides a refuge for ourselves and others from this noisy world.

# Reflect

DO YOU SEEK OR RESIST TIMES OF QUIET? WHY IS THAT? THIS WEEK CARVE OUT A TIME OF QUIET EACH DAY—EVEN IF ONLY FOR A FEW MINUTES. TRY SPENDING THIS TIME IN A DIFFERENT LOCATION EVERY DAY—MAYBE YOUR BACK PORCH OR A PARK BENCH OR A LITTLE NOOK IN YOUR KITCHEN. TAKE NOTE OF WHERE YOUR THOUGHTS WANDER IN THESE MOMENTS OF STILLNESS.

# 48

# Heart Work

Above all else, guard your heart, for
everything you do flows from it.

PROVERBS 4:23

One fateful day in June, I found myself poring over volumes of photos on my computer. I was on a tight project deadline, so naturally, scrolling through the last seven years of photos seemed like the perfect distraction.

As I scrolled, I came across a group of photos I didn't recognize, a series of scenes set in the woods of Connecticut where our family had sought respite over a fall break. Our six-, eight-, and ten-year-olds had dreamed up the perfect kids-will-be-kids afternoon: a picnic by the woods on the edge of the front yard. Gabe had captured the entire experience on camera, lurking behind a curtain in the front office window. I'd had no idea.

Frame by frame, photo by photo, I watched the afternoon unfold in slow motion. Kennedy pitched and batted a solo baseball game, her face awash with sheer determination and grit. Pierce examined a leaf up close, picked from a pile on the ground, then jumped up to cheer for his sister. Cade took their distractions as an opening to finish off lunch, sneaking crumbs to the poodles, who circled nearby.

The next photo caught me off guard. It was me. Head buried in my laptop, headphones on, laser focused on writing my first book. These sacred moments of spontaneity had taken place in the front yard . . . and me? I had missed every second of it.

What other moments had I missed, head buried in my work? I couldn't possibly be present for every one. But this felt different. In that room, seven years later, I fell to my knees in tears.

I suppose most parents live with the question *What more could I have done?* And in that moment, the question came calling for me. Grateful for this insight, I considered a new question: *What can I do now?* This is where things begin to change.

So often, our regret, shame, and self-condemnation do not motivate us to be more present, more proactive. Instead, they lead to more anxiety and defeat. Confession to God, on the other hand, allows us to begin again and make today count. When we pause long enough to examine our hearts, to confess to God where we have messed up, cleansing happens.

> **When we pause long enough to examine our hearts, to confess to God where we have messed up, cleansing happens.**

These things are true: *you cannot heal what is hidden*, but when you confess something out loud, you bring it into the light, where it can be healed. The power of guilt and shame no longer has a hold on you because *secrets lose power when they exit the dark*.[1]

Here are three questions to ask yourself to kick-start the heart work. They will walk you through confession and toward change (which is the path of true repentance).

- *What do I need to confess?*
- *What guilt do I need to release to God's cleansing power?*
- *What do I need to change?*

Guilt and shame keep us trapped in cycles of anxiety, depression, perhaps even panic. The only consistent way I've found rest from these cycles is to keep my heart clean through confession, release, and forgiveness. Let's do the heart work.

# ❧ Reflect ❦

WE MOST OFTEN THINK OF GUARDING THE HEART AS PRO-
TECTING IT FROM EXTERNAL TRAPS AND TEMPTATIONS. HOW
MIGHT IT ALSO MEAN PROTECTING IT FROM OUR OWN GUILT
AND REGRETS? ASK YOURSELF, *WHAT DO I NEED TO CONFESS?*
*WHAT GUILT DO I NEED TO RELEASE?* AND *WHAT DO I NEED TO*
*CHANGE?* JOURNAL YOUR ANSWERS AS WELL AS GOD'S GRACE-
FILLED RESPONSES.

# 49

# Bearing Another's Burdens

Carry each other's burdens, and in this
way you will fulfill the law of Christ.

GALATIANS 6:2

My dad took his final breath in the early morning hours of a Tuesday. When I woke to the finality of the news, I wept in my bed. At dusk, Gabe, my sister, the kids, and I huddled around the living room as family, sharing every memory of Dad we could remember—all the stories I didn't want my children to forget.

The next day I dropped my sister off at the airport and merged onto the interstate for the long drive home. There was a torrential downpour, and when the clouds cracked open, so did my heart, releasing sobs to match the torrent against my windshield. Alone for the first time in three weeks, I was finally free to release my sorrow in tears.

As I drove, my tears reminded me of the story from Scripture of the woman who lost herself in a debt of gratitude when she encountered Jesus. She fell to her knees and tears poured from her, falling all over his feet. Jesus was moved by this sacred outpouring of heartbreak. He praised her for it, blessed her, even said, "Your sins are forgiven."[1] Her tears were the pathway to her healing.

I've never thought of tears as cleansing, but as I drove, my tears were somehow purifying my heart, washing out so much grief and pain. As I cried, it was as if my tears, too, were spilling onto Jesus' feet. I could almost feel the beginnings of healing setting in.

My counselor has a catchphrase: "If you're crying, you're healing." When we allow ourselves to feel, to release, it has positive effects on our emotional state. Crying can be self-soothing and elevate mood better than any antidepressant.[2] It can be our body's natural way to offload stress and anxiety.

The rain and tears provided immediate relief that day, but tears shed in solitude won't ever cure our grief. Waves of depression came knocking for the next two months.

> My counselor has a catchphrase: "If you're crying, you're healing."

But I knew I didn't have to process this pain alone; I could walk through the journey of grief with others. I reached out to my community for impromptu prayer walks, acai-bowl confessions, and front-porch rocking-chair drop-ins. I shared my grief, my tears, and memories of my dad.

Through our consistent time together, I began to pull out of my own pain, and on occasion, the roles shifted. As I shared my burden with them, I invited them to share theirs with me. How were they doing? What were they facing? How could I encourage them?

We weren't designed to beat our fears, our anxieties, and our worries on our own. Meaningful connections help us overcome grief, depression, and sorrow. And once we receive and respond, once we find healing, it's our turn to bear the burdens of others. Together, we find that the burdens of life are somehow bearable, and we find the confidence and strength to overcome.

## ✺ Reflect ✺

IS THERE AN AREA OF YOUR LIFE THAT FEELS HEAVY RIGHT NOW?
IDENTIFY SOMEONE IN YOUR LIFE WHO CAN BE A BURDEN-
BEARER FOR YOU. OR MAYBE YOU'RE DOING OKAY RIGHT NOW.
CONSIDER THOSE WHOSE LIVES LOOK HEAVY, AND ASK HOW
YOU CAN TAKE SOME WEIGHT OFF.

# 50

# Surrendering Power

In my distress I called to the LORD;
I cried to my God for help.
From his temple he heard my voice; my
cry came before him, into his ears.

PSALM 18:6

Cade stood by my bed at four twenty a.m. straining for breath, the harsh noise vibrating so loud it scared him. Tears welled, and his eyes darted back and forth. This was his most severe croup attack at ten years of age. When would they stop?

I leapt out of bed and barreled down the stairs to find a reserve supply of steroids in the fridge. They wouldn't work in time. Gabe was on business thousands of miles away, and Cade and I had minutes to get to the ER. I would leave the younger two in their beds. "God, help!" I called a friend who answered on the first ring. "Please come now."

She was in a cab within two minutes, driving from the west side of the park, so I propped open the front door. Ill-equipped for the chilly, middle-of-the night temps, no jackets, old flip-flops thrown on, Cade cried in my arms through chattering teeth.

Where were all the taxis?

For a brief moment, the desperation transported me to the air above my head. I looked down on us, huddled on a corner of a silent city waiting for a rescue that wouldn't come. "God, surely you won't let us stand here while Cade struggles for breath? With his wide eyes searching mine for help? You love him more than I do. Do something now!"

In moments, a shot of adrenaline pumped into my veins. My eyes locked on Cade's: "You are my brave boy, and we are going to get through this." Stay calm, Mama. He began to relax. Seven minutes later, still no taxi. Cade's breathing became less labored, his tears began to dry and smear.

Finally, I spotted an approaching cab. As I ran toward the car, my friend jumped out. "Thank God, you're here." Cade and I took her place and rushed to the hospital. The cool night air helped Cade take deep gulps, as he faced the open window into the darkness. Healing took place before my eyes. No meds, steroids, or shots. Just hopeful prayers whispered in his ear.

> Healing took place before my eyes. No meds, steroids, or shots. Just hopeful prayers whispered in his ear.

I sat in the waiting room for an hour running my fingers through Cade's hair. His breathing quieted as the silver-haired nurse with kind eyes kept checking on us. Minutes later, they decided he didn't need to be admitted. Cade and I looked at each other and giggled about the miracle moment we had just shared. A smile slid across Cade's cheeks, and he whispered, "Home."

Surrender changes everything, but we don't choose to surrender; it chooses us.

It meets us in our pain, at our lowest point of weariness and longing.

It enters when we have run out of strength, when we believe things may never change.

When our lives feel meaningless, and we break.

How could it be? How could a good God create a life that doesn't matter?

So we cry out and ask for rescue. Deep down we know our own attempts have failed us.

The life we've orchestrated leaves us huddled in despair, in the dark hours of the early morning.

Then we see it. The crack of sunrise, a glow on the horizon.

Pink and orange create a hue that colors the sky.

It's God whispering, "I am here. I am true. I am strength.

"I love you as you are, broken and fragmented. Let me carry you.

"Let me show you a life you never dreamed or imagined.

"Let me take you on a journey so marvelous you point back to me.

"Let me bring you back to your truest self, the way I ordered you from the beginning.

"All this, for my glory."

# ⪧ Reflect ⪦

HAVE YOU HAD MOMENTS IN YOUR LIFE WHEN YOU FELT
COMPLETELY POWERLESS? WHAT HAPPENED NEXT? HOW DID
GOD MEET YOU IN THE SUFFERING? WHAT DID YOU LEARN
ABOUT THE NATURE AND PROVISION OF GOD?

# 51

# Making Memories

Mary treasured up all these things
and pondered them in her heart.

LUKE 2:19

Each year during the holidays, our family pulls out the home movies, loads a bowl with truffle-salt popcorn, and settles in for our absolute favorite trilogy of the year: *Honey, I Shrunk the Kids*; *Honey, I Blew Up the Kids*; and *Star Wars*. No, I'm not talking about the feature films that made over a billion dollars at the box office. I'm talking about the short films inspired by them, starring the Lyons family, circa 2006–2007.

As new parents in our twenties with almost no energy to spare, Gabe and I received some valuable advice from Mark and Jan Foreman, our mentors and friends, who had managed to raise their kids to become creative adults. Mark and Jan championed one big idea: when our children come to us with a crazy

> **When our children come to us with a crazy idea of an experience they'd like to create, our answer should always be yes.**

idea of an experience they'd like to create, our answer should always be yes.

At age four Pierce wanted to make films, and what better place to start than our basement? The first short film would be *Honey, I Blew Up the Kids.* Cade was the baby, Kennedy was the babysitter, Pierce was the professor, and Gabe and I were, well, the parents. The growing machine was our vacuum with its detachable suction tube and the Hot Wheels cars and racetrack made up the city once Cade was blown up. In five short minutes, after terrorizing the faux city, Cade was shrunk back down to a normal size and reunited with his mom and dad in our minivan in the garage, all while the cameras kept rolling.

Then came the Luke Skywalker lightsaber phase. Wearing a sash, my brown western boots, and a fuzzy eye mask strapped around his head for a beard, five-year-old Pierce played Luke. I was Princess Leia with two braided side buns and a white bathrobe. Cade was the villain in a voice-activated Darth Vader helmet and Gabe's black coat. My favorite scene is the finale, where Luke brags to Leia how he was "pushin' 'im and shovin' 'im" (Darth) until victory was won, all while drinking a can of Coke.

Saying yes became the way we engaged with our children. It challenged us to be creative, even when they asked for improbable experiences like making feature films. But it also offered me something just as valuable—especially on rough days when I didn't feel like getting out of bed. I was motivated to push apathy to the side as Pierce or Kennedy or Cade asked me to join in their wild creativity.

Imagination precedes creativity.[1] When we break out of the cycle of drudgery and focus on creating memories with those around us, we start to find the wonder in life.

The next time you find yourself at the end of a difficult week, instead of disengaging or escaping, what if you made a memory? What if you completed some kind of family project or made a family film? What if you baked Christmas cookies in July or created a silly new game? Making memories helps us step outside ourselves, even if just for a moment. In seasons of great stress or anxiety, it might be the very thing that turns everything around.

# ❦ Reflect ❦

ARE YOU FEELING STUCK IN AN ENDLESS LOOP OF TO-DO LISTS? WHEN WAS THE LAST TIME YOU SAID YES TO SOMETHING CREATIVE AND FUN? MAKE A MEMORY THIS WEEK. AND ONCE IT'S MADE, TAKE NOTE OF HOW IT MADE YOU—AND THOSE YOU LOVE—FEEL.

# 52

# Celebrate Freedom

You, my brothers and sisters, were
called to be free. But do not use your
freedom to indulge [yourselves]; rather,
serve one another humbly in love.

GALATIANS 5:13

These things I know:

Freedom begets freedom.

Freedom is contagious.

Freedom helps us set others free.

It's true. Paul wrote that it is for freedom that we have been set free, that we should not carry the yoke of slavery any longer.[1] But Paul didn't stop there. He continued, explaining *how* to live once we are free. "Do not use your freedom to indulge [your-selves]; rather, serve one another humbly in love."[2]

God wants us to use our freedom for the good of others.

When my own journey to freedom in Christ began, I carried all kinds of weight—self-sufficiency and arrogance, guilt and shame. One day I told Jesus I felt like my brokenness was too great. Maybe I'd thwart his plans for my life. Instantly, I heard, "What if your purpose is for me to love you?" What could I say to that? No performing, no achievement, no success, and no amount of devoted effort can earn the love of Christ.

Knowing this, when the fears came, I held fast to the words of Paul:

"Don't run back to the yoke of slavery."[3]

*Don't run back.*

*The cell door is open.*

*Run free!*

No matter what you've experienced, the pain you've felt, the victimization you've encountered. When God feels far away, *do you see it?*

*Confession is the gateway to freedom.*

> **Confession is the gateway to freedom.**

That's it. Every time. This isn't a one-time, "sinner's prayer" kind of thing. This is an Every-Moment-You're-about-to-Lose-Your-Crazy kind of thing. There's no brilliant formula for being a super-Christian. We are all broken and in desperate need of a Savior.

We are *nothing* without him.

We are *everything* in him.

Three years ago, I asked Jesus to take my heart "back to where it was free and alive and so deliriously joyful it could burst," and that's exactly what he did. I've been set free to confess, to thirst, to ask, to begin again, to step into my calling, to wait, to grieve, to be weak, to be brave, to rest, to celebrate, and to love.

But this freedom isn't just for me. It's for you too. Jesus knew you before you were formed in your mother's womb. He had a purpose for your freedom, even before the beginning of time. He sought you with his everlasting love. Even when you struggle to believe his promises, he'll free you, fill you, heal you, and satisfy your soul. He'll redeem what was broken. Then he'll equip you to tell your story—his story—so that you might set others free. Freedom is never just for the freed. Freedom is a gift that's meant to be shared.

You are invaluable to the kingdom of heaven. God has appointed a specific role only you can play. You are needed and wanted, chosen and set apart, beloved and worthy. You will receive all power and glory when the Spirit comes on you. You will bear witness to everything Christ did to set you free.

This is your calling. You are free. Go. Set others free.

# Reflect

PRAY FOR MOMENTS TO TALK ABOUT WHAT GOD HAS DONE IN YOUR LIFE. PRAY FOR FRIENDS WHO DON'T KNOW THE LORD, AND ASK THAT THEIR HEARTS WOULD BE SOFTENED. ARE THERE PLACES IN YOUR LIFE WHERE YOU CONCEAL YOUR FAITH? CONSIDER WHAT IT WOULD LOOK LIKE TO BE MORE OPEN ABOUT FOLLOWING HIM, AND PRAY AMONG FRIENDS FOR THE CONFIDENCE TO DO SO.

# Notes

## Chapter 2: Healing Joy

1. Luke 19:10.
2. From a lecture Eugene Peterson gave to a group of Q attendees in New York City, 2011.

## Chapter 3: Living Water

1. John 4:1–34 (paraphrased).

## Chapter 4: Declaring Truth

1. From the New King James Version.
2. Romans 8:2.
3. Romans 8:17; Galatians 4:4–5.
4. Titus 3:4–7.
5. Hebrews 12:29.

6. Romans 8:38–39.

7. Galatians 5:1.

8. See 1 Corinthians 6:20; Galatians 3:13.

## Chapter 6: Asking the Impossible

1. Matthew 17:20; Luke 17:6.

2. Luke 11:10.

## Chapter 7: Simply Brave

1. Deuteronomy 31:6.

2. Mark 9:23.

3. Philippians 4:13.

4. Philippians 1:6.

## Chapter 9: God's Surprises

1. Exodus 4:1–13.

2. Hebrews 13:20–21.

3. 2 Corinthians 12:9–10.

## Chapter 10: Letting Go

1. Psalm 23:1 NKJV.

## Chapter 15: Being Whole

1. Romans 8:28 (paraphrased).

## Chapter 18: Pulling Weeds

1. Ephesians 4:11–12.

## Chapter 21: Expressing Your Emotions

1. This wisdom was shared with Gabe by a counselor named Al Andrews.
2. John 11:33–35.
3. Luke 19:41–22.
4. Matthew 26:37–38 NLT.

## Chapter 22: Strength in Weakness

1. 1 Corinthians 11:28.
2. 1 Corinthians 11:30–32.

## Chapter 23: Rhythms of Sleep

1. Arianna Huffington, *The Sleep Revolution: Transforming Your Life, One Night at a Time* (New York: Harmony Books, 2016), 28.

## Chapter 24: A Little Sweat

1. Ashish Sharma, Vishal Madaan, and Frederick D. Petty, "Exercise for Mental Health," *The Primary Care Companion to the Journal of Clinical Psychiatry* 8, no. 2 (2006): 106, https://www.ncbi.nlm.nih.gov/pmc/articles/PMC1470658/.
2. Jo Barton and Jules Pretty, "What Is the Best Dose of Nature and Green Exercise for Improving Mental Health? A Multi-Study Analysis," *Environmental Science and Technology* 44,

no. 10 (March 2010): https://texanbynature.org/wp-content/
uploads/2016/10/What-is-the-Best-Dose-of-Nature-and-Gre . . .
-Mental-Health-A-Multi-Study-Analysis.pdf.

## Chapter 25: Confession for Your Soul
1. From Ann's keynote address at the 2013 Allume Conference.
2. *Cambridge Dictionary of American English* (Cambridge, 2007), s.v.
   "confession."

## Chapter 27: Taking a Walk
1. "Seasonal Affective Disorder," National Institute of Mental
   Health, https://www.nimh.nih.gov/health/topics/seasonal-
   affective-disorder/index.shtml.
2. Nilofer Merchant, "Sitting Is the Smoking of Our Generation,"
   *Harvard Business Review*, January 14, 2013, https://hbr.
   org/2013/01/sitting-is-the-smoking-of-our-generation.

## Chapter 31: Dreaming Dreams
1. Viktor Frankl, *Man's Search for Meaning* (Boston, MA: Beacon
   Press, 1959), 165.
2. Galatians 5:14 THE MESSAGE.

## Chapter 33: Taking a Risk
1. Matthew 6:34.

Chapter 35: New Learning
1. Julia Cameron, "The Road Less Travelled: Artist Date Suggestion," *The Artist's Way*, January 4 2012, https://juliacameronlive.com/2012/01/04/33437/.

Chapter 36: Holy Inventory
1. Parker J. Palmer, *Let Your Life Speak* (San Francisco, CA: Jossey-Bass, 2009), 1.
2. Psalm 139:16.
3. Ephesians 3:20.

Chapter 38: Your Calling
1. Psalm 139:13–14.
2. Psalm 139:15–16.

Chapter 40: The Way of Forgiveness
1. Ephesians 4:26–27.

Chapter 41: The Gift of Hugs
1. Luke 7:45; 18:15–17.

Chapter 42: I'm Sorry
1. Ephesians 4:26–27.
2. John 10:10.

## Chapter 46: True Connection

1. Emma Seppala, "Connectedness & Health: The Science of Social Connection," The Center for Compassion and Altruism Research and Education, Stanford Medicine, May 8, 2014, http://ccare. stanford.edu/uncategorized/connectedness-health-the-science-of-social-connection-infographic/.
2. Hebrews 10:24–25.

## Chapter 47: A Quiet Stillness

1. Susan Cain, *Quiet: The Power of Introverts in a World That Can't Stop Talking* (New York: Crown Publishers, 2012), 11.
2. Author Emerson Eggerichs stated this to Gabe and me when we spent time with him in marriage counseling. He said most people think the key to a great marriage is "good communication," but this is false. The key to a great marriage is mutual understanding.

## Chapter 48: Heart Work

1. Ephesians 5:13; James 5:16.

## Chapter 49: Bearing Another's Burdens

1. Luke 7:48.
2. Asmir Gračanin, Lauren M. Bylsma, and Ad J. J. M. Vingerhoets, "Is Crying a Self-Soothing Behavior?" *Frontiers in Psychology* 5 (May 2014), https://www.ncbi.nlm.nih.gov/pmc/articles/PMC4035568/.

3. Chapter 51: Making Memories

1. Dan Hunter, "Imagination Precedes Creativity," *You Can Only Imagine* (blog), H-IQ, July 6, 2017, https://hunter-iq.com/imagination-precedes-creativity/.

Chapter 52: Celebrate Freedom

1. Galatians 5:1.
2. Galatians 5:13.
3. Galatians 5:1 (paraphrased).

# About the Author

Rebekah Lyons is a national speaker, host of the *Rhythms for Life* podcast, and bestselling author of *Rhythms of Renewal*, *You Are Free*, and *Freefall to Fly*. An old soul with a contemporary, honest voice, Rebekah reveals her own battles to overcome anxiety and depression—and invites others to discover and boldly pursue their God-given purpose. Alongside her husband, Gabe, Rebekah finds joy in raising four children, two of whom have Down syndrome. She wears her heart on her sleeve, a benefit to friends and readers alike. Her work has been featured on the *TODAY* show, *Good Morning America*, CNN, FOX News, *Publishers Weekly Starred Reviews*, and more.

The *Rhythms of Renewal* book and *Rhythms of Renewal Study Guide with DVD* are your guides to daily rescue.

Daily struggles with anxiety and stress make it difficult to receive God's peace. *Rhythms of Renewal* will help you trade your anxiety for the vibrant life you were meant to live through four profound rhythms: rest, restore, connect, and create. With encouraging stories and practical steps, Rebekah Lyons will help you begin an intentional, lifelong journey toward sustained emotional, relational, and spiritual health.

## Rest, Restore, Connect, and Create with the *Rhythms for Life Planner and Journal*

For anyone who struggles with stress, anxiety, overcommitment, depression, or exhaustion, here's the next right step. The perfect companion to the bestselling *Rhythms of Renewal* by Rebekah Lyons, this beautiful journaling planner is exactly what you need to build restorative rhythms into your daily routine for a life of health, purpose, and joy.

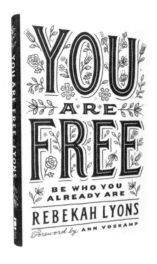

Discover that freedom is for everyone who wants it in the *You Are Free* book and *You Are Free Study Guide with DVD*

You don't have to keep striving for freedom; live in the freedom you already have in Christ. In these pages, Rebekah Lyons walks you through her journey of releasing stress, anxiety, and worry to uncover the peace that is offered to us through Jesus Christ.